Passion for Love and Happiness

by

Dr. A. A. Syed
M.B.B.S., F.R.C.P.(C), F.A.C.P.

COVER TO COVER PUBLICATIONS

2009

ISBN
978-0-9784368-2-7

Published by:
Cover to Cover Publications
3 Engleburn Place
Peterborough, ON Canada
K9H 1C4

705-745-2868
ketaylor@covertocover.ca

About the Author

I was born in Hyderabad India in 1956. My father was a government servant, and his main aim was for his children to have a good education. I have one older sister, an elder brother, and one younger sister. I went to a private Catholic school in Hyderabad from 1960 to 1972. From 1972 to 1974, I joined the premedical program of New Science College in Hyderabad. I went to medical school from 1975 to 1980 (Gandhi Medical College / Osmania University). I married my childhood sweetheart, Syeda, in 1981 and migrated to Canada in 1982. I then went into the community medicine/internal medicine residency program for postgraduate education at the University of Alberta in Edmonton, staying there until 1984, when I moved to the University of Saskatchewan (Saskatoon) to take up first an internal medicine residency and fellowship and then a respirology fellowship. I have been a fellow of the Royal College of Physicians of Canada (FRCP [C]) since 1988. I have had American Board of Internal Medicine Certification since 1986, and, since 1991, I have been a fellow of the American College of Physicians (F.A.C.P.).

I moved to Lindsay, Ontario in 1988, which is a town of 23,000 that is about 125 km north of Toronto. I have been practicing here ever since as a specialist in internal medicine, respirology, and critical care medicine. I have been Chief of Medicine, as well as Chief of Intensive Care Medicine, at Ross Memorial Hospital in Lindsay for several years, and I am currently practicing as a consultant in respirology and internal medicine.

My hobbies have always been sports. I was the table tennis champion of Hyderabad India for 2 years, and India's number three player for another 2 years. I was also on the team that represented India in an international tournament. Currently, I play golf and have a handicap of around 15. I also play tennis in my spare time. I have always had an interest in reading books, and have recently read books on human psychology.

I was encouraged by family and friends to write this first book on love and happiness. The research that went into the writing of this book has taught me a lot, and I would like to, in turn, share it with you.

I have been married to Syeda for the last 28 years. She has been my biggest supporter. We have three lovely children—Noreen, age 25, who is married and currently completing her master's degree in science and physiotherapy; Nazeen, age 22, who will be doing her MBA this fall; and my son, Imran, who is 14 and going to high school in Lindsay.

I have travelled extensively in India while playing table tennis tournaments, and I've seen the best and worst of life in India. I have travelled extensively by train, from first class to third class compartments, and I have seen the country's historic places. I have seen extreme poverty as well. I am from an average family. My father had just enough money to put his children through private school, as education was his prime objective for his children. I learned a great deal from my father. He made me understand how life should be lived, and I am still trying to follow his teachings, even though he has passed away.

My father was my guru in this field of human behaviour and philosophy. I will always cherish the time I had with him, and also with my loving mother who has given me a great deal of love and affection.

Dr. A. A. Syed

Acknowledgements

I thank my wife, Syeda, to whom I have been married for 28 years, for her patience, support, and the encouragement to write this book.

I thank Carolyn (Fallis) Hale for her help in research and proofreading this book, even though she had to deal with her diagnosis of cancer.

I thank my editor, Karen Taylor, for doing a wonderful job in editing this book. Without her help, I could not have published this book.

I would like to thank my publisher, Cover To Cover Publication Services – Karen and Louis Taylor – for contributing a great deal of their time and effort in publishing this book. I personally thank Karen, my editor, for doing an excellent job. She was always there to improve my book with a lot of patience. I also personally would like to thank Louis Taylor for the layout, design and cover of the book.

Dr. A. A. Syed

TABLE OF CONTENTS

Dedication

I dedicate this book, *Passion for Love and Happiness,* in loving memory of my father, who inspired me to write this book. He was a perfect example of unconditional love.

FOREWORD

This is my first book—*Passion For Love and Happiness.* I always cherished good fortune, and I would like to share with you my views and thoughts about life. The basic thing, which I have learned, is that you have to be content to be happy. This book is designed to offer you a strategy to help you live and enjoy life with contentment and happiness. I will be reviewing some of the fundamentals since "repetition is the mother of skill." I hope this is a book you will read again and again, using it as a tool to trigger yourself to find the answers that lie within yourself. Remember that, as you read this book, you do not have to believe or use everything in it. Just grab a few things that you think are useful and put them into action. You will see how your life changes. You won't have to implement all the strategies or tools in this book to make a sea change in your life.

In this book, I have taken messages—in the form of poetry and quotations—from our saints and saviours, wise individuals who have lived on this planet over the last few thousand years. They have left us with these great messages to improve our lives. I have always been fascinated by saints and saviours, such as Buddha, Jesus Christ, and the Prophet Mohammed, who have left such great messages showing us how to be happy and content. I am also impressed by the teachers, philosophers, theologians, and poets who have lived on this earth for the last few hundred years. They, too, have left us some great spiritual messages, which will improve our lives if we listen. Their poetry and quotations are also utilized throughout this book. I have given my own thoughts about these messages and written commentaries on these quotations and poems about contentment and happiness.

Over 2,500 years of literature, from the time of Buddha, through the time of Jesus Christ and the Prophet Mohammed, and up to recent times, has been surveyed to find insight. I have taken the wisdom of writers and philosophers in the form of poetry and prose and commented on the thought-provoking life lessons of Lao Tzu, Confucius, Zen proverbs, Rumi, Sir Edward Dyer, Alexander Pope, William Blake, Elizabeth Barrett Browning, Henry David Thoreau, Ralph Waldo Emerson, Robert Browning, Walt Whitman, Steven Crane, Kahlil Gibran, Rabindranath Tagore, Mahatma Gandhi, George Bernard Shaw, e. e. cummings, Martin Luther King, Jr., Mother Theresa, and many others. I have also included the wisdom of currently living people, such as the Dalai Lama, Wayne Dyer, Dr. Deepak Chopra, Richard Carlson, and Anthony Robbins.

I have utilized these quotations from the books and teachings on contentment and happiness, and I have written my own views. I am hopeful that you will read this book again and again to bring about a change in yourself and to help you live a contented and happy life.

I have also used the words of many other philosophers, theologians, poets, mathematicians, as well as quotations from the Holy Bible, for example, from Corinthians and Matthew, and from the Hadith (the teachings of the Prophet Mohammed). There are also insights from other great people who have lived on this earth, including Socrates, Aristotle, Ayn Rand, René Descartes, Aldous Huxley, Michel de Montaigne, Thomas Fuller, Jeremy Bentham, Albert Einstein, Archimedes, Edmund Spenser, Henry Ward Beecher, Joseph Conrad, John Locke, John Gooden, André Gide, Mark Twain, Emmett Fox, Mencius, Seneca, and Benjamin Disraeli.

These are the great people who have lived in another age on this earth; they have left us some amazing spiritual messages in the form of poetry and prose, and these messages concern what is so important in today's life. Implement these messages in your lives to make life happy and content.

This book is full of strategies for achieving success in the nurturing of contentment and happiness, and it contains organizing principles that I have modelled from some of the most powerful encounters I have had—with people of different cultures from the East and the West. Also, from within my profession as a medical doctor dealing with very sick people and their families, I have derived principles about how to cope with sorrow as well as how to delve the depths within to find ways to be content and happy.

The purpose of this book is not just to help you make a singular change in your life; rather, it is meant to be a pivot point that can assist you in turning your life around, in taking your entire life to a new level. You can understand the basic human nature and spirit that we all have within: our inner contentment and happiness. By reading this book again and again, you will learn to make changes in your life and overcome phobias and fears and improve the quality of your relationships. As you read, you will find that there are key points within your life when, if you make a small change, it will literally transform every aspect of your life.

I am not sharing this book with you on the pretence that I have all the answers or that my life has been perfect. I have most certainly had my share of challenges and problems. However, I have managed to learn and continuously succeed. Each time I met a challenge, I used what I had learned to take my life to a new level. I would like you to learn from this book what I have learned—how to expand and grow, how to become a good human being and have passion for contentment and happiness.

Living my life may not be the answer for you, and my dreams and goals may not be yours, but I believe that the lessons I have learned—how to turn dreams into reality and how to take the intangible and make it real—are fundamental in achieving any level of inner growth. I am writing this book as an action guide and a textbook for improving the quality of life by paying more attention to contentment and happiness. I firmly believe that our quality of life will be much better if we are content and happy. With this in mind, I have started this book with great respect and with the consideration that I am beginning to have a relationship with you and that we will start together on a journey of discovery of our deepest and truest potential. Life is a gift and offers us the privilege, responsibility, and opportunity to give something back by becoming something more ourselves.

So let us begin our journey by exploring the depth of inner contentment, which leads to inner happiness.

Dr. A. A. Syed
May 4, 2009

CHAPTER 1

Love and Relationships

The spiritual evolution of a person is achieved by a disciplined mind. I think that the backbone of discipline is the element that provides the motive and the energy for discipline. It is a force of love. If the love is too deep, too large and, truly, if we want to understand and measure it, the limited framework of words prevents us. But, I will try my best to define love in this chapter on love and relationships.

To my knowledge, the mysterious nature of love has not been defined in a very true and satisfactory fashion in literature. All have tried to explain it in their own way. I will make an effort to explain, in my way, what love is and to give a simple definition of love, again with the awareness that this definition is likely to be inadequate. I define love as an extension of our own self for the purpose of nurturing our own spiritual and mental growth. You may notice that this is a theological definition of love, and the behaviour is defined in terms of personal spiritual inner growth.

In the evolutionary process of the development of self, one has to successfully extend one's limits and then grow into a larger being. This act of loving is an act of self-evolution. Therefore, the definition of love includes self love and love for others. Because we are human beings, we are dedicated to human spiritual development; as a part of the human race, we are dedicated to our own development as well as to the development of others in the human race. But it is important to love ourselves first because only then can we love others. Just as we are incapable of teaching our children self discipline if we, ourselves, are not self-disciplined, for the sake of spiritual growth, one has to love one's self before loving others. We cannot be a source of strength unless we nurture our own inner growth and inner strength. As we explore the nature of love, it will become clear that we have to learn not only self-love but also to love others. Ultimately, this will be indistinguishable. Love is an act of will, namely, an act of intention as well as an act of action. It is also important to note that we do not have to love to lust. It is our choice to love, no matter how much we think we are loving. On the other hand, when we do exert ourselves in the cause of spiritual growth, we choose to love, and we will grow spiritually.

Patients who are referred for psychotherapy are mostly confused about the nature of love. There are a lot of misconceptions about love, which will be discussed in this book. The suffering seems to be unnecessary because these popular misconceptions can be made unpopular through the teaching of more precise definitions of love.

Misconceptions of Love

The most powerful belief and misconception about love concerns falling in love. It is a very potent misconception because falling in love is a subjective experience in a very powerful fashion, as is the experience of love itself. When a person falls in love, that person feels that she or he loves someone, but the problems are immediately apparent. The first is that the experience of falling in love is linked to sex or to an erotic experience. We fall in love only when we are consciously or unconsciously sexually active and motivated. The second problem is that the experience of falling in love is invariably quite temporary, no matter with whom we fall in love. Sooner or later, we fall out of love if the relationship continues long enough, and we invariably cease loving the person with whom we fell in love because, once the feeling of ecstatic lovingness has gone, then the experience of falling in love always diminishes and passes away. The honeymoon period is over, and the bloom of romance gradually fades, and the ecstatic love we had gradually fades as we fall out of love.

To understand the phenomenon of falling in and out of love, it is necessary to understand the nature of what psychologists call "ego boundaries." A newborn infant, during the first few months of its life, does not distinguish between itself and the rest of the world. As the infant gradually grows and sees the mother or another caregiver, then the baby gradually learns about the world. Initially, the infant cannot distinguish himself from the parents, and there is no distinction between him and the world. There are no boundaries, no separations, and no identity. But, as the child grows and experiences himself as an entity separate from the rest of the world, his behaviour changes and a sense of "me" begins to develop as the interaction between the infant and the parent gradually grows. The child begins to have a sense of his own identity. When the interaction between the caregiver and the child is disturbed, for example when a child's mother has no satisfactorily loving and caring attitude, then we see mental illness in the development of that infant, whose sense of identity is grossly defective in the most basic ways. The distinction of identity, the separateness of the child's self compared to the rest of the world is distorted in the very early stages of infancy if the infant does not receive satisfactory love and affection from the mother or the mother-like substitute.

When the infant grows in the first year of her life, she begins to distinguish between herself and the world. In the first year, she knows that the body parts like legs, arms, and voice belongs to her. She begins to gradually note her physical limits, and these are called "boundaries". The knowledge of these limits is set in each child's mind. These are called "ego boundaries."

The development of ego boundaries is a process that continues throughout childhood into adolescence, and even into adulthood. When the boundaries are established in later years, more psychological problems are encountered in those individuals. For instance, between the ages of two and three is typically the time when the child comes to terms with the limits of his power. Up to the age of two, the child usually tries to command the mother's attention, trying to expand his ego boundaries. He can act like a tyrant trying to give orders to parents, siblings and other family members, even family pets. In his mind, these entities belong to him. When he does not get the proper response, he will act out, as much as possible, to expand these ego boundaries. These are the "terrible twos" that we are all aware of.

By the end of age three, the child has come to grips with and knows about her ego boundaries because some of her acts have not been acceptable to the rest of the family. She then gradually knows her relative powerlessness and gradually comes to grips with the situation and accepts it. But, if this child is allowed to do whatever she pleases, then the possibility of omnipotence is so great and sweet that it cannot be completely given up for several years. This child may have distorted ego boundaries and will have problems in future years. The normal child of age three generally comes to accept the reality of the boundaries of her power. Sometimes she may try to escape, for some years, into the world of fantasy in which the possibility of omnipotence, particularly her own, exists. This is the time when characters such as Superman and Tarzan are appealing. She gradually gives up the super heroes, and, by the time of mid-adolescence, the child is confined to the boundaries that limit the individual's power. Children know their ego boundaries quite well by then, and try to fit into a group we call society. In this group, they are not particularly distinguishable, yet they are isolated from other individuals by their own boundaries, identities, and limits.

Behind these boundaries, some people are particularly lonely. These are the people who have schizoid personalities. They have had unpleasant, traumatizing experiences in childhood. These are the people who perceive the world outside themselves as dangerous, hostile, confusing, and unpleasant. These people have boundaries that are so self-containing that they find comfort and a sense of security in their loneliness.

For most of us who have had normal development, loneliness is quite painful. We always want to escape from the world of loneliness and try to unify ourselves with the rest of the world. The experience of falling in love allows us to escape temporally, and the sense of falling in love is occasioned by a sudden collapse of the individual's ego boundaries, permitting a person to merge his or her identify with that of the loved one. The sudden release of one's self from one's self and the exposure of one's self to the other, with whom we have fallen in love, create quite a dramatic experience. It is a release from loneliness. The dramatic release from loneliness accompanying the collapse of ego boundaries is experienced by most of us as a very ecstatic experience—as becoming one with our beloved. Our loneliness no longer exists.

Some psychologists call the act of falling in love an act of regression. The experience of merging with a loved one has its roots in our genes—in the fact that we were merged with our mothers in the first nine months of our existence. Along with merging, we also re-experience, in the act of falling in love, the sense of our omnipotence, which we had to give up in our journey out of childhood. When we are united with our beloved, we feel we can conquer all of the world's obstacles, and we believe that the strength of our love will cause the force of nature to bow down in submission and melt away somehow. All problems in life look easy, and we think we can overcome anything. The future looks very bright. The feelings we have when we fall in love are essentially the same as the unrealistic thoughts of two-year-old children who feel themselves to be the kings of the world with unlimited power. Love, or rather being in love, presents itself in a person's having unrealistic expectations of his or her partner; a person in love feels omnipotent, just as a child does.

The truth intrudes on the two-year-olds fantasy of omnipotence, as it does on our fantastic fantasy of falling in love. Sooner or later, responses to the problems of daily living creep into the relationship, and these responses show the real self. For instance, he wants to have sex, and she is not in the mood to have it. She wants to put money in the bank, and he wants a new television set. She wants to talk about her family, but he wants to talk about his friends. In the privacy of the heart, they begin to come to a true realization that they are not one with their partner and that each partner has her or his own ego boundaries. Their desires, prejudices, and tastes are different. One by one, gradually or suddenly, the ego boundaries snap back into place and gradually or suddenly, they fall out of love. Once again, they are two separate individuals who have their own needs and requirements. They have their own ego boundaries. The point is, when they realize that this has occurred, they dissolve the ties created by falling in love. Once again, they are two separate and different individuals. At this point, two things can happen. Either they break the ties of their relationship, or they initiate to work towards a real loving relationship.

In a real loving relationship, one must understand that the perception of falling in love is actually a false perception, that the subjective sense of loving our beloved is actually an illusion. This illusion of love will be discussed later in this book. The true act of loving actually comes out of our inner self during our inner spiritual growth. However, by stating that these loving feelings occur when a couple falls in love and that they then disappear rather quickly when the couple falls out of love, we now question what real love is, implying that love does not have its roots in the feeling of falling in love. To the contrary, real love often exists at a different level in a different context in which the feeling of love is from deep within our spiritual self.

Therefore, falling in love is not real, for several reasons. Falling in love is not an act of our inner will. It is not a conscious choice but rather a matter of how eager we are, at a particular time, when we meet someone who attracts us sexually. It is an elusive experience, as we are quite likely to fall in love with someone with whom we are obviously ill matched or with someone who is not well suited to our nature. Falling in love is not an extension of one's ego boundaries but is actually a partial, temporary collapse of ego boundaries as a person gets lonely or is sexually attracted to another. The extension of one's limits requires effort and discipline. Real love needs discipline as well as spiritual and mental growth. Lazy and undisciplined individuals are quite likely to fall in love (and to fall in love often) because they experience solace in becoming one with another, in losing their ego boundaries to get rid of their loneliness or to fulfil their sexual pride. Once the moment of falling in love has passed and the boundaries of an individual's persona have snapped back into place, then this individual may be disillusioned by this experience.

Real love is about permanently growing and self-enlarging our selves. Falling in love is not real love but rather just a collapse of ego boundaries. The person actually goes into regression, into the infant stage of development when, because of having an insecure mind, he or she wants to be one with another.

Falling in love has little to do with nurturing our beloved's progress or with the development of one's own spiritual growth. It is a way to terminate our own loneliness. Unsuccessful marriages can result from falling in love as an antidote to loneliness because these marriages do not enable self-actualization or extension. When we fall in love, we do not feel ourselves to be in need of any spiritual or inner growth. We are totally content with who we are, where we are, and with the person we love. We are at peace, and we do not perceive our beloved as being in any need of inner growth or spiritual growth either. On the contrary, we perceive our beloved to be perfect in every sense. Even if we see some flaws in our beloved, we perceive these to be insignificant, little eccentricities of our darling love, and these only add colour and charm to this temporary situation of falling in love.

Falling in love, as I mentioned, is the temporary and partial collapse of our ego boundaries. The sexual specificity of this falling in love phenomenon makes us suspect that it is a genetically determined occurrence, intended for allowing a person to meet someone with whom he or she might have children. In other words, it is a mating behaviour that is engrained in our genes. In other words, the temporary collapse of boundaries that constitutes falling in love is actually a stereotypical response of human beings to their internal sexual drives and also to external sexual stimuli, and falling in love serves the probability of sexual pairing, sexual bonding, and sexual activity to enhance the survival of the species.

Falling in love, then, is a trick of nature, which pulls our genes to do the work of nature and to get "hooked" to the beloved. This feeling of falling in love can trap us into bonding and marriage. This trick of nature, which is actually an illusion, can temporarily move us into regression to an infantile stage. We merge with our omnipotence, and many of us end up in a marriage, which is usually temporary. Over 50 per cent of these marriages end in divorce.

Romantic Love

Romantic love is actually an illusion that is deeply engrained in our culture by commonly held love stories and fairytales, such as Snow White and Cinderella. The prince and princess, once united in marriage, live happily ever after. The myth about romantic love is that each young man or young woman in this world thinks that there is somebody out there who is meant for him or her and that, one day, the couple will meet and be united forever. Another myth is that there is only one man meant for one woman, and vice versa. Some believe that a person's true love is predetermined in the sky, in the stars, and when the lovers meet, they will recognize each other on sight and fall in love. The match is made in heaven, which is a perfect match. The belief is that each member of a couple will fulfil the other member's needs, and therefore they both will live happily ever after in perfect harmony, in a perfect union.

We often see the opposite happen. One day, when marriage partners do not satisfy each other's needs, the friction arises, and, very quickly, they fall out of love. They realize that their romantic love was a dreadful mistake, although they thought it to have been made in the heavens, skies, and stars. Their marriage was not only an imperfect match but also their love was not real or true love; what brought these two into a union of marriage was nothing but vibrating genes creating mutual hormonal attraction and causing what seemed to be a very romantic love. Once two people are united in marriage and this mistake is realized, that the love which was thought to be real was not a real love or a true love, nothing can be done about the situation except that either they have to live very unhappily ever after or get a divorce.

The myth of romantic love is actually a very dreadful lie. It is probably a very necessary lie in that it ensures the survival of the species by encouraging and validating the falling in love experience that traps the couple into marriage.

Psychiatrists see this in their practices everyday—the confusion and suffering caused by the myths of falling in love and finding romantic love. Millions of people waste their energy desperately attempting to make the reality of their lives conform to the unrealistic myth of romantic love. For example, Mrs. C, married for 2 years, becomes severely depressed without any apparent cause and enters into psychotherapy. As she says to her psychiatrist, "I don't know what is wrong. I have everything I need and also a very perfect marriage." Only after a few months does she accept the fact that she has fallen out of love with her husband for obvious reasons as these two are different individuals with different likes and dislikes and different ego boundaries, as I mentioned earlier.

Another example is Mr. D, who, after being married for 2 years, begins to get chest pain periodically, which is atypical in nature. He has a thorough examination by a cardiologist to find out that his chest pains are not due to a cardiac problem but rather are related to stress. He later gets psychotherapy and admits to the psychiatrist that his wife bugs the hell out of him by always wanting to buy everything and by having no respect or regard for the amount of money he makes. We can go on with a number of examples like Mr. D and Mrs. C. Each has fallen out of love and realized that falling in romantic love was a miserable mistake. Both realize that they are very different people from their spouses, with different interests. They are no longer romantically in love with their partners but are still committed to their relationships. They are clinging to the myth and attempting to conform their lives to this horrible myth of romantic love. They may state that, even though they have fallen out of love, they will act, through sheer will power, as if they are still in love. Then maybe, they think, romantic love will return to their lives in the future, but this usually does not happen. These couples go to psychotherapy to find out what exactly went wrong in their marriage. The psychiatrist probably tells them they are too married and too closely coupled. Each will have to establish his or her own psychological distance from the other, as they are two very separate and different individuals with their own likes and dislikes and ego boundaries. Sometimes, it is necessary to separate them physically during their group therapy, and sometimes it is necessary to stop them from speaking for each other by saying, "Let your husband speak for himself" or "Let your wife speak for herself."

Therefore, I believe falling in romantic love is an illusion, which does not constitute real love.

If falling in love is not reality, then what is real love?

Real love has to do with ego boundaries. We have to extend our ego boundaries to experience real love. What I mean by extending ego boundaries is extending ourselves to a level where we reach out towards our beloved, whose mental and spiritual growth we always wish to nurture along with our own mental and spiritual inner growth. For this to happen, our beloved must first become attracted to us and invested in and committed to us in every way, and he or she must be especially dedicated to extending our mutual boundaries of self. This process of attraction, investment, and commitment is also called "cathexis." The word *cathexis* is related to the word *cathect*, which means to attract the beloved object and invest emotional energy in it, and, when we cathect an object of our love that is outside of ourselves, we are then psychologically incorporating that object into ourselves. For example, a man who gardens as a hobby loves his garden so much that he is totally attracted to or cathected in the garden and finds it attractive. He has totally invested himself in and committed to his garden—he may jump out of bed early in the mornings to get to his garden, refuse to travel any distance from it, and even neglect his family. The process of cathexis requires him to nurture the shrubs and flowers in his garden. Despite the knowledge that the garden exists outside of him, it has become a part of him through this cathexis, through his investment in the garden's nurturing. By loving his garden so much, he has incorporated the garden into himself. This incorporation leads to the man being enlarged and to his ego boundaries being extended: his ego now includes the entity of his love, that is, his garden, which has become a part of him.

In the real love of any object, we extend our ego boundaries and go with the cathexis of our extension, which is actually a progressive enlargement of our self and incorporation of our self within this world. We grow by stretching our ego boundaries. In this way, the more we extend the self, the more we love, and the more we begin to learn the distinction between the self and the world. We now become identified with the world as our ego boundaries become blurred and thin. Then, as we let go of our ego boundaries, we begin to experience the same sort of ecstatic feeling as we did when we fell in love and these ego boundaries partially collapsed. Instead of having merged temporarily into an unrealistic, single, deliberate object, however, we have now merged realistically into the world. This is a mystical union with the entire world. The feeling of ecstasy or bliss, which is associated with this union, is fantastic and wonderful. It is a similar feeling to that of falling in love, but it is established on a more permanent basis. It is more stable and lasting. Ultimately, it is very satisfying. This is what we call real love, and we achieve it by extending our own ego boundaries to experience the whole world with true or real love. The difference between the peak experience typified by falling in love and what Abraham Maslow has referred to as the "plateau" experience is that, with the latter, "The heights are not suddenly glimpsed and lost. They are attained forever."[1]

Love and sexual activity may occur simultaneously, but they are two different phenomena, and they are totally dissociated. Making love, itself, is not an act of love. The experience of sexual intercourse, particularly an orgasm or even masturbation, is an experience associated with at least some degree (greater or lesser) of a collapse of ego boundaries and the attainment of ecstasy at that moment. It is because of this collapse of the ego boundaries that people may shout at the moment of climax "I love you" or "Oh, God" to whomever they are with, be it their spouse, significant other, a stranger, or even a prostitute. Once that moment is gone, the ego boundaries snap back into place. We may feel no threat of attraction to that other person. This is not to say that the ecstasy of orgasmic experience cannot be heightened by sharing it with a loving partner, but, without such a partner, the collapse of ego boundaries in conjunction with orgasm may be total but only for a second. We totally forget who we are. We lose track and are lost in time and space. We are outside our world and outside ourselves. We are transported to a different plane where we become united with the whole universe. However, this feeling lasts only for a few seconds, for the time during which we experience this ecstasy of making love and having an orgasm.

The point here is that this ecstasy of the orgasm is the same experience as unifying one's self with the universe, with our source, which is associated with an orgasm. However, a prolonged association or oneness with the universe (or with the source), a union that is associated with real love, is so much more momentous compared to the fleeting feeling of oneness achieved during orgasm, which is only for a few seconds. The mystical union of real love, by which we become one with the universe or source, is essentially a belief that happens when one has real love; it is a belief in the unity of all things, in the reality of oneness. This reality of oneness is experienced in the most literal sense; the mystics believe that the common perception of the universe as comprised of multiple, discreet objects, such as people, animals, trees, planets, stars, moons, and the sun, all separated from one another by their own boundaries is actually a misconception or misperception. It is an illusion. This misperception in the Hindu and Buddhist religions is called *Maya*. Some mystics believe that true reality can be known only by experience. The oneness is known through giving up our egos and our ego boundaries to become one with the universe or source. Then, and only then, can we really see the unity of the universe, as long as we continue to see our selves not as discreet, separate objects but rather as part of this universe or source. This can only be felt with real love, when a person lets go of his or her ego and becomes one with the universe and source.

Hindus and Buddhists have a belief that an infant, before the development of ego boundaries, knows reality. It is also mentioned in the Holy Bible that a child is one with the heavens. Because children do not know their ego boundaries, they are with the source while we adults develop ego boundaries of self and separate ourselves from the universe and its source. Some mystics even suggest that the path towards enlightenment or knowledge is actually a oneness with reality that requires us to regress to a child-like state and become as infants, losing our ego boundaries and becoming one with the source.

> Except ye be converted and become as little children, ye shall not enter into the Kingdom of Heaven.
> *Jesus of Nazareth*[2]

There is an eternal child in each one of us. As ageless children, we become synonymous with heaven, which represents eternity without any boundaries. Jesus is telling us that we should be child-like and not childish and live life with great enthusiasm. The word enthusiasm is derived from a Greek word, enthousiasmos, that ultimately comes from the Greek adjective entheos, which means "having God within." When we live like an ageless child, which is within us, life is eternal and has no boundaries of ego. We live with enthusiasm without hatred or judgment. In a child, there is nothing to judge and no one to hate, as the child does not have ego boundaries and recognizes no distinctions because of appearances. It only knows how to look at everyone with pure and genuine love. A child with no ego boundaries is an absolute allower. It allows everything to unfold naturally, an unfolding of God in every one of us. This is what being an "ageless child" means: being that which resides in each one of us and does not distinguish colour, size, shape, or any personality. To the child, there is no distinction between ethnic or cultural variations. Therefore, the ageless child is always at peace, and it only observes. It only allows. The invisible child in us all, to whom Jesus refers, is always non-judgmental, loving, accepting, and is not capable of placing any labels on anyone. We should realize that, in every adult, there is a child who desperately wants to come out. This child is full of enthusiasm or God-like feeling. A child is one with the universe and the source. The adult who is usually empty has developed an ego. Adults are judgmental and have fears and anxieties. The child is, in fact, enlightened, as there is purity in the child's divine love of the heavens, and God within. Children have God's acceptance. This is what is known as a "ticket to heaven"; the little children enter the Kingdom of Heaven, as do adults who have converted to child-like purity. The key here is being converted—when we become child-like and lose our ego boundaries, we become one with the source. Then, we do not have any judgments, fears, or anxieties. We are perfect, kind, loving, and, above all, we become eternal with the universe and the source.

When we become child-like, we leave behind the childish attitudes of an adult. This helps us to enter the Kingdom of Heaven, as is written in the Bible. The Kingdom of Heaven is available to all of us on this planet. I believe it is here on earth that we reap what we sow and make and pay for our mistakes. Here, on this planet, we can make our own heaven of becoming child-like, with no ego boundaries. We can become one with the universe and the source. This is what I believe can be achieved with real, genuine love.

Most mystics understand this truth. The infant, without its ego boundaries, may be closer in touch with reality than its parents. However, it is incapable of surviving without the care from its parents. It is incapable of communicating this wisdom to the world. The path to sainthood, then, must go through adulthood. There are no easy short cuts. The ego has to be hardened first and then it has to be softened by letting go of it. This can only be achieved by real love.

The temporal release from ego boundaries is associated, as I mentioned, with falling in love or with sexual intercourse. Even using certain psychedelic drugs can give people a glimpse of the ecstasy of reaching Nirvana. However, this glimpse is not the real Nirvana itself. Nirvana means lasting enlightenment or true spiritual and mental growth. And true lasting enlightenment or Nirvana can only be achieved through the persistent exercise of real love—by permanently losing the ego self or ego boundaries and becoming one with the universe and the source.

The temporary loss of ego boundaries is seen when we fall in love and during sexual intercourse. Both experiences lead us not only to make commitments to other people from which real love may begin but also to gain insight into a mystical ecstasy of love that is everlasting. This mystical ecstasy of love is the same feeling of love that we glimpse momentarily during the first passions of romantic love or during orgasm, but it is always present and permanent. It is everlasting feeling. This true and lasting love can only be achieved by releasing our ego self or ego boundaries, by feeling the association of our selves with the universe and the source—from which we have come.

Dependency In Love

The next most common misconception about love concerns dependency of love. Psychologists and psychotherapists deal with this problem on a daily basis as they see individuals who become depressed in response to being rejected by or separated from their spouses or loved ones. These people have a tendency to believe that they cannot live without their spouses, loved ones—whomever they think they love. They say they are completely lost without them. Their lives, they believe, have no meaning without the other people, with whom they believe they are desperately in love. This is called dependency of love.

I feel that it is nothing more than our own insecure minds, which leads to this dependency of love. This desperate need is not real or true love. When a person requires another person for survival, then I do not think that person has understood the deep meaning of love. This kind of love is a matter of necessity. It does not have any free will or the freedom of choice. When two people love each other, they should be quite capable of living without each other.

Dependency in love in a healthy individual is definitely a pathological state. It is a manifestation of mental illness. We all depend somewhat on our spouses. We want, now and then, to be babied or nurtured by our loved one. However, when a person feels that she or he just cannot live without the other person, that he or she is madly in love with the other person, this only indicates an insecure state of mind.

Most of us have desires and feelings, but these should not rule our lives. When they do rule our lives and dictate the quality of our lives, then we have something more than just dependency needs. Those whose lives are ruled and dictated by dependency needs may suffer from a psychiatric disorder called *passive-dependent personality disorder*. It is one of the most common psychiatric disorders seen in day-to-day psychiatry practices.

People who suffer from passive-dependent personality disorder are so busy seeking to be loved that they do not have any energy left to actually love someone. They are the people who are starving for love because of their dependency needs, which are occasioned by their own inner emptiness. They are the ones crying out from their bottomless pit because their dependency needs never get fulfilled. They always feel there is something missing from their lives. These are the people who can never tolerate loneliness. Because they lack a real sense of identity, these people define themselves solely through the dependent love relationship. But, it is never fulfilling. They are always dependent on their spouse, telling their spouse that, without a doubt, it is only with their love that can they live. But, this is a misconception of love. It is, as I said, parasitism, living off of the person loved.

These people usually do not have long-lasting relationships. Their relationships change rapidly as their dependency needs change. Their relationships seem quite intense and dramatic. But, they are actually quite shallow. Because of their inner emptiness and hunger to fill it, these passive-dependent people cannot delay gratification of their own needs.

This passive dependency is commonly seen in young women between the ages of 17 and 24 who have an endless series of sexual relationships with men beneath their own intelligence. They usually go from one loser to the next, as their own love dependency is not met. The word *passive* is used in association with the word *dependent* because these individuals are so concerned about themselves that they usually do not care about the people they think they love. Their needs are totally dependent upon the other person. These dependent passive people never do things for others, but rather their motive is to do things to cement the attachment of the other person whom they think they are in love with, so their own care is assured. These are the people who find it hard to live on their own, separate from their parents, for example, or to buy a house on their own or get a job. They usually have unsatisfactory jobs, and they usually do not have any hobbies.

The inner feeling of emptiness in these individuals usually has its genesis in the lack of love they experienced during childhood. The parents of these individuals are responsible for not having given their children enough attention and affection, which are required in early development for mental growth. Children who are loved and cared for with consistency throughout their childhood enter adulthood with a deep-seated feeling that they are lovable people and are valuable and, therefore, will be loved and cared for as long as they are true to themselves and also others. Children who grew up in an atmosphere where love was lacking in the family have gross inconsistencies in their behaviour in adulthood and a sense of inner insecurity. This inner sense of insecurity is a feeling that they do not have enough, so the experience a dependent need. They scramble for love, care, and attention whenever and wherever they can find these things. Once they have found love, care, or attention, then they are desperate not to let go of it. They have a manipulative type of behaviour in hanging on to their so-called "true love." They claim they could never live without the other person, as they think they are deeply and truly in love with that person. But, their dependent need is not love of the other person. Instead, the excessive dependency of the passive-dependent person is a lack of inner self-discipline. They are unwilling to delay gratification, and they are in desperation to form and preserve attachments. They are not honest with themselves. Because of their dependency, they cling to failing relationships when they should give them up. They lack a sense of responsibility for themselves. They are passively looking for others to fulfil their own dependency needs. Therefore, when they are not fulfilled or happy, they feel that others are responsible for their misfortunes. They see even their own children as a source of their unhappiness and unfulfilling life. Consequently, they are angry and are endlessly let down by others. They cannot find a real and fulfilling relationship.

In a healthy marriage, there is normally a differentiation of the roles of the two spouses. In the olden days, the woman would do all of the housework, and the men would work to make a living. But now, things have changed, and both of them often must work outside the home. A good, strong marriage can only exist between two strong independent people who care and love each other. Dependency does not make for a healthy marriage.

Dependency in love may appear to be true love, but it is not. It is a form of anti-love or parasitism. It has its genesis in parental failure to love their children in early childhood. It always seeks to receive rather than give. It leads to infantilism rather than growth. It destroys relationships rather than builds them. It usually constricts rather than liberates.

Dependency in love is not connected at all to spiritual growth. The people who are dependent, saying they love someone because of their own insecurities, are always looking for their own nourishment. They desire filling their own selves, and they have no desire to grow spiritually. They are unwilling to tolerate any unhappiness or loneliness. Dependent people do not care about their own spiritual growth or that of the people they think they love. They care only that the one they think they love is there to satisfy their demands. Dependency is a form of behaviour that is uncharacteristically applied to the word love. I think real or true love is usually concerned with the spiritual growth of one's self and also the spiritual growth of the person who is truly loved. This means we care about the other person and care about that person's happiness and inner spiritual and mental growth.

And what of the person who fills the needs of a dependent individual? Does this person show love? No. When we truly love someone, we do not simply give, but rather love is judicious giving, judicious praising, and judicious criticizing. It is also judicious struggling, converting, pushing, pulling, or guiding, and it is a type of leadership that we have in ourselves and direct towards the mental and spiritual growth of the person we love. The word *judicious* means judged with a will, that is, not with our instinct. This judicious development of self and loved one is done with thoughtfulness and also requires, sometimes, painful decision making. This is what I call love for one's self, which leads to personal mental and spiritual growth. Also, with this kind of attitude, we can make a difference in the mental and spiritual growth of the people we truly love.

On the other hand, the motives behind injudicious giving or nurturing are destructive, and the giver, under the disguise of love, is responding to and meeting his or her own needs without any regard to the spiritual growth of the receiver. Injudicious giving leads to self-sacrifice. This is a misguided love.

It is a serious perversion of love that is also called *masochism*. People untrained in psychology or philosophy tend to associate sadism and masochism with purely sexual activities, thinking that both pathologies involve inflicting or receiving physical pain during sexual involvement. True sexual sadism or masochism is a relatively uncommon form of psychopathology, but general sadism or masochism is a much more common phenomenon. Social sadism and masochism can lead people to unconsciously desire to hurt others or themselves through entering a non-sexual interpersonal relationship of dominance or self-sacrifice.

The issue of social masochism raises another major misconception about love and that is that love means self-sacrifice. The prototypical social masochist equates love and self-sacrifice. Although this person appears to be directly motivated by the needs of another, she or he is dependent on responding to these needs in order to maintain the image of herself or himself as a loving and caring individual who makes any sacrifice for love. But this is not true love.

When we genuinely love, we do so because we want to love sincerely, from deep within ourselves. It is true that love involves a change in ourselves. But, this change is an extension of our self rather than the sacrificing of our self. Love is always self-replenishing; it enlarges us rather than diminish us. It fills the self with love rather than depleting the self of love. Genuine love always aims for the mental and spiritual growth of our self and the mental and spiritual growth of the person we truly love.

The Feeling of Love

The feeling of love is an emotion that accompanies our attraction to the other person, our cathexing to or investing emotion in the other person. Cathexing, as I mentioned earlier, is a process in which we are attracted to the other person and so concentrate our libido or emotional energy on that person. But we may be attracted at that particular moment in time for any reason; that is, our attraction may be either sexual or one of friendship, but it is not a true feeling of love. It is just cathexing, as we cathex even to an inanimate object like jewellery, money, or the stock market. The fact is, we have been attracted to invest emotion in another, but this does not mean we feel love or that we have fallen in love with the other person or with an inanimate object, such as money, jewellery, or pets, as I mentioned. It is not a true feeling of love. Finally, once the cathexis or attraction is over, any feeling of love may also end. For instance, say two people meet in a bar, and they are sexually attracted to each other. Once their sexual consummation is over, the two may find each other undesirable or unattractive. They may experience decathexis (the withdrawal of emotional attachment or libido) and be unattracted to each other. So cathexis or attraction is not a feeling of love.

On the other hand, genuine love implies commitment and wisdom. When we love someone genuinely, we want that person to have mental and spiritual growth. We know that a lack of commitment without genuine love would be harmful for any real feeling of love. In a genuine and constructive marriage, just as in any other constructive and real long-term relationship, the partners must routinely and regularly attend to each other's needs with a real feeling of genuine love. Only then will the relationship between the two individuals bloom. Couples sooner or later fall in and out of love, as I mentioned, when they are only attracted or cathexed to each other because of mating instincts. If they do not have an opportunity for genuine love to begin and bloom and improve, then this needy relationship does not last long.

Genuine love transcends the matter of attraction or cathexis. When real love exists, it does so without attraction or cathexis, with a feeling of true love. It is a true, deep, inner, genuine feeling of love that will gradually develop if we are totally committed to our beloved and have a deep desire for the mental and spiritual growth of that individual. Genuine love is true love, which extends one's self for the purpose of nurturing our own spiritual growth as well as the spiritual and mental growth of our beloved. The person who genuinely loves does so because they have the will to love. The key word here is *will*. This person has made a commitment to his or her beloved not because that person is attracted or experiences cathexis or has a loving feeling but because of a much deeper act of will, a true commitment derived from genuine love, which exercises total control of the person's feelings and always brings with it a deep inner desire for real improvement in the spiritual and mental growth of the beloved. True love is not just a feeling of love; it is much deeper than that. It is a commitment and a thoughtful decision of the will as well as the desire to love the other person. A common tendency is to confuse love with a feeling of love, as I mentioned previously. The feeling of love is nothing but an attraction towards the other person or cathexis to the other person. True or genuine love is an act of will that transcends the feeling of love or attraction or cathexis. It is always correct to say that love is as love does. Love is always good and always improves our mental and spiritual growth.

The Will to Love

> When we analyze will with all the tools modern psychoanalysis brings us, we shall find ourselves pushed back to the level of attention or intention as the seat of will. The effort which goes into the exercise of the will is really effort of attention; the strain in willing is the effort to keep the consciousness clear, i.e., the strain of keeping the attention focused.
>
> *Rollo May*[3]

Love is an act of will. It is work against the inertia of our own minds. Love requires work and courage directed towards the nurturing of our own and another person's mental and spiritual growth. We have to exert courage in directing the spiritual growth of our self and of our beloved, of the people we truly love. This courage requires an act of will. Since it requires an extension of our own self, love is always an act of will with courage. When we love ourselves, we always attend to our own inner growth. When we truly love others, then we care for their inner growth. This requires an act of will and true courage.

The most important way in which we can exercise our love is by having true attention and willingness to listen to the people we love with open ears. Listening requires will and attention as well as courage. Many of us have no ears to hear or time to listen to the people we supposedly love. As one psychologist points out, the amount of time we devote to teaching certain subjects to our children in school is inversely proportional to the frequency with which the children will make use of the subject when they grow up. A business executive will probably spend hours in a day talking and not listening. In school, also, a large amount of time is spent teaching children to read and a very small amount of time is spent teaching children how to speak and how to listen. I think the world would be wiser if we had lessons in the schools, and in our homes, to teach our children how to listen. Learning to listen is more important than learning the ABCs, for example. Listening well, with open ears, is an exercise of attention. It definitely requires courage and hard work. We do not realize that because we are not willing to listen to the people we love; and not listening creates enormous problems in our day-to-day lives, and with those who share our lives.

Recently, I went to a spiritual conference where one of the speakers was very good. He was speaking on a topic of interest to me. This brilliant scholar gave considerable insight into how to know God. It was a well-attended lecture by this God-seeking audience. During the coffee break, there were a lot of comments regarding this philosopher and scholar. Many people were disappointed in his lecture, knowing his reputation. They were expecting more from him, I suppose. They found him confusing and had difficulty following his points. Compared to other lectures, this one spoke to me. I was able to hear exactly what this great man was saying precisely because I was willing to do the work of listening to him. I was willing to do this work of listening for two reasons. First, I recognized that this man really had a deep vision into the topic on which he was speaking. Second, I was very interested in the topic he was discussing. I was deeply absorbed in his lecture, wanting to enhance my own understanding of my inner spiritual growth. I loved him because I perceived him to be a great person, and I knew his lecture was worth attending. I loved myself because I was willing to work on my own behalf toward my own personal inner growth. My love was primarily self-directed and motivated by what I could get out of this relationship between teacher and pupil. He was also rewarded because probably only a few people in the audience understood his message, and I had because of my deep concentration and attention and my love for the particular topic he was speaking about. There was growth for me, as well as a reward for the teacher who was trying to convey his message on that particular topic.

As you will see, love is a two-way street. We have to have a reciprocal relationship between the giver and the receiver of love.

Listening with total concentration is a manifestation of love. True listening is a discipline of bracketing, that is, temporarily giving up of our self and setting aside our own prejudices and desires so as to experience, as much as possible, the speaker's point of view and stepping into that person's psyche. The unification of the listener and the speaker is actually an extension and enlargement of our self. New knowledge is gained from this manoeuvre. The energy required for this discipline of bracketing, when we set aside our selves giving more importance and total acceptance to another, along with the total concentration of our listening, opens up a dance of love between the speaker and the listener. The energy required for bracketing and for focusing total attention is only accomplished by the will of love and by extending ourselves for the mutual growth of both the listener and the speaker. Many people lack this energy. We may lack it, even though we may feel that, in our daily dealings and social circles or businesses, we are listening very hard. However, usually very few people learn the art of listening. Because of my experience as a physician, I have developed a habit of listening with total concentration to the patient's complaints; one of my old teachers who taught me clinical medicine told me that, after taking a good history, a doctor will usually (up to 90 percent of the time) be able to diagnose a disease by thorough concentration and listening to the patient's complaints. Only 10 percent of the time is a true diagnosis made by examining a patient and doing diagnostic tests. In clinical medicine, it is very important to get a good history of a person's experiences and symptoms of a disease by listening to the patient with total concentration. Sometimes you have to guide patients with proper questions, but, a lot of the time, it is just the art of listening, through the will of love, which enables a doctor to help that patient and to make a proper diagnosis. Physicians who lack the art of listening to their patients lose the patients' trust. Some patients who have been referred to me by their family physicians tell me that their family doctor does not listen to what they are saying and therefore is unable to make the proper diagnosis. Consequently, they have been referred to me to help them. It is not uncommon, in the medical practice of a specialist, that the patient is referred for further investigative work and diagnosis. But many family physicians, who see their patients frequently, sometimes do not have the ears to listen to the same complaints again and again. They lose track of where they are and are unable to make a proper diagnosis. At that point, they may refer that patient to a specialist who can help in making the proper diagnosis of that patient. In my practice, it is very important to listen to my patients' complaints, taking a thorough history with full attention and with total focus, with the intention of healing the patient with true love in my heart. Listening goes a long way toward building a good relationship of confidence between me and the patient, as well as toward my making a proper diagnosis.

True listening is true love. It is very appropriate for a couple that wishes to remain happily married. We all know it is very important to listen. Yet, many an individual in a supposedly loving relationship does not truly listen to his or her beloved. True listening can occur only when you set aside time for it and build the conditions that are supportive of it. It cannot occur when someone is too tired, too anxious, or doing a household activity. But, it will happen if you truly set aside time for your spouse and listen to him or her. The results are very gratifying. The joy is real when you have the will to listen to your spouse. This has to come from deep within. It all indicates true love for your spouse. Falling in love is effortless. But couples should frequently shoulder the effort and discipline of true loving and listening. The knowledge that one is being truly listened to is very therapeutic. It improves marital relationships.

True love with your spouse requires courage. Courage can be without fear. It is an action that moves against resistance and is not generated by fear of the unknown. This courage will lead to spiritual growth and, therefore, true love for our spouse.

Love and Inner Growth

Growing up requires stepping from childhood into adulthood. It is often a fearful leap rather than just a step. It is a leap that many people do not take during their lifetime. Though they may appear to be adults, even successful adults, the majority of grownups remain in their psychological childhood patterns of attitudes. They have never truly separated themselves from their parents or from the power their parents had over them in their childhood. The growing up process requires very gradual, multiple little leaps into the unknown, such as when an 8-year-old learns to skate or ski or ride a bicycle or a 16-year-old goes out on a first date. These actions represent real risks, and, definitely, there is a pattern of anxiety involved in taking these little leaps into the unknown. Healthy children, when they grow into adulthood and take on adult activities, experience some reluctance and may cling to safe and familiar ground, sometimes holding on to the dependency of childhood. But as a child takes these risks, the child gradually becomes the adult. Sometimes, however, children encounter considerable danger when growing up, so they feel unable to take any additional risk. Other children are taught to fear any risk at all. Children in both situations may retain child-like attitudes into adulthood and can consequently experience psychiatric or psychological problems. These adults who have not developed psychologically, who have not taken leaps into the unknown, are not motivated. Primarily, their parents usually have a similar background and have an over-protective attitude. These adults are stuck in the childhood phase of growth and require approval, or even disapproval, from their parents, even if the parents have long since died. Psychologically these child-like adults are never there to take their destiny into their own hands, as their fear of the future and of the unknown keeps them in the childhood phase of mental and inner growth.

Most of us have to take great leaps into the future, mainly in adolescence. By the age of 30–35, most of are married, and we have children. We have a balanced life if we grow out of childhood attitudes and take leaps into adulthood. Such leaps into independence and self-determination are painful at any age, and they require courage.

We should ask ourselves, what does growing up have to do with love? I believe it is very important. Until we have self-love, we cannot grow up mentally and spiritually. We cannot take leaps into the future and into the unknown. It is self-love that lets us face the future with courage, and it requires courage to make major changes in our lives, to go ahead and take the risks involved, which leads to inner spiritual growth.

Consider my case. I am from an average family. I grew up in India, with all of the financial problems that are common in that country. My parents were very loving. They encouraged us; especially my father always encouraged me to be brave and take leaps into the future and into the unknown. This was engrained in my psyche from a very young age. I remember travelling alone on trains, in second- or third-class compartments, at the age of 12 when I was playing table tennis at a sub-junior level in many different competitions. My parents never discouraged me and always encouraged me to be on my own. Therefore, I had no fear of the future or of the unknown. I always took risks. When I became an adolescent, I had the opportunity to go to South Korea to be on the Indian team at the age of 16, to represent India in an Asian junior table tennis championship. At that point, I had to make a decision: whether to take up table tennis as a profession and become a professional table tennis player or get into premedical sciences and become a doctor. The decision was completely up to me. My father encouraged me to be a doctor, but the ultimate decision was mine. He guided me, saying that my future as a professional table tennis player would not be as good as it would if I were to become a medical doctor. I took this leap into the unknown and did not go to Seoul, South Korea for the junior table tennis championships. At that time, it was quite painful for me to give up this big opportunity to represent my country in the tournament. But, at the same time, my decision was very important because I had to write my premedical examination so that I could get into medical school. I took this leap into the future with courage, wrote all of the exams, and got into medical school. When I made the decision to stay in India and study, I was not sure whether I could even get into medical school, but I was sure I could have gone to play in the international table tennis tournament in South Korea. But this was an important decision and a courageous one, especially for a 16-year-old young man. To choose something more important and more fulfilling but more risky—trying to become a medical doctor—rather than remaining in India and playing table tennis as a professional table tennis player was difficult for a 16-year-old so much in love with the game of table tennis. To give up such an opportunity was painful. However, the courage to take the risk involved in making the decision to study for medical school was also important. The self-love I had and the courage I had made me make that important decision at that critical time. Looking back, I believe it was a wise decision that I made when I was young and growing from adolescence into adulthood. I took a great leap into an unknown. I have been, so far, greatly rewarded for making such a good decision at such a young age. This is why self-love is so important; it gives you courage. That courage, in turn, will make you a better human being. We all have to make major decisions at different stages of our lives. But, if you have self-love, you will make the right decision for yourself. Taking the risk involved in jumping into the unknown can be done wisely when you have self-love.

When I made that decision, I felt I was probably making the wrong decision, or a crazy decision, because I was not sure whether I could even pass the medical entrance examinations. The exams were so very difficult, and I was very much involved in table tennis. I had to give up the game I loved and study for the exams. Ultimately, I did get into medical school. It was daring. It was different. I felt it was a crazy time for me, but I was responding to the loving messages from my parents, probably hundreds of them sent during my childhood. Their words of encouragement are always in my mind: "You are a great human being" or "You are beautiful" and "You are loving" and "No matter what, you will make the right decision for yourself, which will carve your destiny." I believe that it was my parents' love that led me to have self-love. This has given me the courage to make the right decisions. Their message to me, at that time, was that they would love me no matter what decision I made. Without the security of my parents' love, which was expressed in myself as self-love, I could not have chosen well because I could not have risked making a wrong decision. The decisions I ultimately made were the right decisions for me. Because of their love, and my own self-love, my leap into the future was done with great courage. When one who has self-love takes a leap into the unknown, there is psychological independence and the development of a unique individuality. We feel that we are free to proceed along to higher levels of inner and spiritual growth, and we are free to manifest love in every way and perform in great dimensions. The greatest commitment is to the self first—to have self-love, which leads to inner mental and spiritual growth. Only then we will have love for everyone else—for our spouses, our children, our parents, our families, our friends, our colleagues, and the rest of the world.

Love is Commitment

> Our sense of commitment, after the wedding, makes possible the transition from falling in love to genuine love. It is our commitment, after conception, which transforms us from biological into psychological parents.
> *Joseph Goldstein*[4]

Commitment is the foundation of genuine love. Deep commitment does not promise that the relationship will succeed, but, at least, it will bolster it. Sometimes, shallow commitments may grow into deep commitments if the relationship lasts a long time. I have mentioned that falling in love is not real love, but, at least, it can be the beginning of love, as it blissfully blinds a pair into taking the risk of having a relationship that can take the form of bonding and marriage. When we are concerned with the spiritual growth of our self and our spouse, then, consciously, we foster the growth of a relationship through commitment. We know very well that children cannot grow into mature adults when there is unpredictability and lack of commitment in a marriage. Couples cannot resolve issues of dependence and independence, submission and dominance, fertility and freedom without the security of knowing that there is commitment in the relationship.

People with character disorders tend to form very shallow commitments. They lack the capacity to form long-term relationships because they fear the risk of commitment. The parents of these individuals often did not have a meaningful relationship with their young children because they lacked commitment to their children. Neurotics, on the other hand, are aware of the need for commitment but frequently have a fear of committing themselves because their early childhood was one in which, although their parents were sufficiently committed to them, they lacked parental love and affection. Neurotics experience a lack of parental love through the death of a parent, chronic rejection by a parent, or abandonment, which leads to intolerable pain during their childhood and adolescence. This pain leads these people into a neurotic state.

When I was growing up, fortunately, I had the total commitment of genuine love from my parents. There are four children in our family. As siblings growing up, we all had love and affection at home. The credit goes to my parents, who suffered through financial troubles but still had the commitment to put us through a private Catholic school where there was discipline so that we could get a good education. Education with discipline,

I believe, is the cornerstone of the inner growth, mental or spiritual, of an individual.

I have been married to my wife Syeda for the last 28 years. I knew her when she was a child, and we interacted as children. We are actually distantly related. She used to go to a girl's private school, which was beside my school. Sometimes, I used to walk back with her to her home after school, and I remember sometimes her father used to give us a ride in his very old car, which I had to push when it stopped to get it started again! It was so funny that her father was always looking for people to give a lift to. But the fact is that this old car would stop, and he would need a little push to get it started again. I remember, also that, as children, we used to dread getting a lift from her father because we always had to push his car so frequently on the way home.

I was 20 years old when I started medical school after doing my premedical education. I was seriously looking for somebody to be my future bride. At that point, I think I probably fell in love with Syeda. When I was in my first year of medical school, Syeda's parents migrated to Canada. Because I had known her since childhood, I knew that she matched me in many ways because of our temperaments, so I proposed to her, and she accepted my proposal. We waited another five years before I could come to Canada, after finishing medical school, to marry her.

In my heart, I had committed to her, and my love for her gradually grew, even though we were separated those five years. I knew she also had love in her heart for me for those five years, and she had committed to getting married when I finished medical school. I think our true love started to bloom after we got married, however. We had committed to each other, and, somewhere along the line, we fell in love with each other. Once we were bound in marriage, we accepted each other's individuality and each other's temperaments, which are quite unique for each of us. With this acceptance in our hearts, that we are two separate individuals with our own ego boundaries, we worked our way in this marriage with total commitment to each other, and we are now full of love, which I think is true and genuine love, a love that gradually grew over the years.

We moved to Edmonton, Alberta in 1982, after we got married in October 1981. I got my first residency training position in the University of Alberta in social and preventative medicine, and, after that, I switched to internal medicine. We spent two years of residency training in Edmonton, where Noreen was born in 1984. From there, we moved to Saskatchewan, as I was offered a residency in internal medicine, followed by a fellowship in pulmonary medicine. For the next four years, we lived in Saskatchewan, first in Regina and then in Saskatoon, where my second daughter, Nazneen, was born in 1986.

I finished my specialization in internal medicine and pulmonary medicine. We moved to Lindsay, Ontario in 1988, and, since then, I have been practicing here as a respirologist, doing critical care medicine at Ross Memorial Hospital.

My son Imran was born on Christmas Day in 1994 in Lindsay, Ontario. He is a bundle of joy. He is unique in many ways and very different from his sisters. All three of my children have very different personalities, and they are unique individuals. They are separate in many ways, and all of them are doing very well in their schools and careers. The commitment of the love of parents for their children is very important. The children see its significance when they are very young. This commitment of love is engrained in children's minds and takes children a long way from childhood into adulthood: they know that the security of a loving family is so important in the mental and spiritual growth of children, in the journey from childhood to adulthood.

During these years, my wife and I committed to each other and to our love, which I think is true and genuine love, and our love has gradually grown with this commitment, as we know we are separate individuals. We have our own unique individualities. We accept each other as different people, but, still, we care about our own and one another's inner mental and spiritual growth because we care and truly love each other. We have our own likes and dislikes. I truly dislike going to a mall and shopping all day, but Syeda, on the other hand, loves to shop for the whole day. I love to golf all day, but Syeda hardly golfs at all. She will go out with me once in a while, but I won't stay on a golf course for more than an hour or two when she is with me. We have accepted each other's separateness, uniqueness, and different temperaments, but the most important thing is the total commitment we have to each other for our own inner mental and spiritual growth. We have total commitment for our children, too, who see us suffer with them when they are suffering. They also see the thrill and enjoyment we experience when they are successful in their endeavours.

As I look back, my own inner mental and spiritual growth has to do with the mental and spiritual growth of my family members. I have always looked for a meaningful relationship with them, and I have changed my own self over the years, making room for a better self, which led to my own mental and spiritual growth. As I mentioned, the discipline of bracketing (of honestly focussing on another and listening) requires an extension of self—

a changing of our self to a better self. With our own improving, enlarging self, we always look for the improvement and enlargement of those other selves we love, for the spiritual and mental growth of our loved ones, for example, our immediate family members. This can happen with total commitment of love. This is what I call good parenting as well as good psychotherapy: when we have a bracketing and extension of ourselves and are enlarging ourselves with the commitment of improving and enlarging the members our family through love and commitment.

As parents, we have to listen to our children by responding to their needs. We have to change ourselves over time to accommodate them. Only when we are willing to undergo the suffering of such a change can we become good parents to our children. Children are constantly growing, and their needs constantly change. We are obliged to grow and change with them. The same principle of bracketing involves undergoing a change in ourselves and accepting our children's needs, as we change for a better self. For instance, some parents can deal effectively with their adolescent children but become totally ineffective as parents while their children are going from adolescence to adulthood; the attitudes of these parents may not change, and they want their children to be young and listen to them. This is not love. This is an insecure mind that does not have the commitment of love needed to be changing and bracketing to a new self and accepting the changes in children growing from adolescence to adulthood. Those parents who do not change or bracket suffer. I think that commitment and love, along with the suffering and changing involved in good parenting, do not add up to martyrdom or self-sacrifice. To the contrary, I think that parents who bracket, or change and evolve with their children, gain a lot through their own inner mental and spiritual growth. Parents who are unwilling to risk the changes involved in growing and learning along with their children are actually choosing a path to senility. These parents leave the real and ever-changing world behind. As parents, learning from our children is the best opportunity we have to assure ourselves of a meaningful old age.

The poem of Kahlil Gibran from his book *The Prophet* goes very well here, and I would like to share it with you. These are, in my opinion, the finest words in literature ever written about raising children.

> Your children are not your children.
> They are the sons and daughters of Life's longing for itself.
> They come through you but not from you,
> And though they are with you yet they belong not to you.

You may give them your love but not your thoughts,
For they have their own thoughts.
You may house their bodies but not their souls,
For their souls dwell in the house of tomorrow, which you cannot visit,
not even in your dreams.
You may strive to be like them, but seek not to make them like you.
For life goes not backward nor tarries with yesterday.
You are the bows from which your children as living arrows are sent forth.
The archer sees the mark upon the path of the infinite, and
He bends you with His might that His arrows may go swift and far.
Let your bending in the Archer's hand be for gladness;
For even as He loves the arrow that flies, so He loves also the bow that
is stable. [5]

Parents who do not seem to have an appreciation of the separateness of those to whom they are close, such as their children, interfere not only with their grown children's parenting efforts but also with their children's intimate relationships, such as marriage.

The necessity of separateness in any close relationship has been a true problem of humans through the ages. It is not just in a marriage or family situation that we have to accept the separateness of the individual but also in the politics. Communism, for example, is a philosophy not of separateness but of the togetherness of a group. Because, in communism, the purpose and function is to serve the community or the country and, as a group, individuals have to be unified and not separate, communism is gradually fading away from this world.

On the other hand, pure capitalism involves the destiny of the individual at the expense of the individual's relationship with a group and, collectively, with society. The sad part of pure capitalism is that the poor suffer, but the separate, unique individual entrepreneur enjoys the fruits of his or her hard work. There are no easy solutions to the problem of separateness from a family, society, or country, but it is quite important that the uniqueness and separateness of individuals be endorsed by a culture for its people to have a happy, healthy society.

Marriages cannot be successful if individuals are terrified by their loneliness. Genuine love not only respects the individuality and uniqueness of the spouse but actually cultivates this uniqueness and risks the separateness of the spouse as necessary for achieving the ultimate goal of married life—being able to grow together mentally and spiritually. That can only be accomplished if you accept the separateness and uniqueness of your partner. The ultimate goal of life is a solitary journey to the peaks. These can be climbed alone, but we should, given the nature of our own individuality, also nurture the separateness of our spouse, who is making an independent but parallel climb. Only then will a successful marriage lead to a successful family, which will lead to a successful society.

As I mentioned, all genuine love requires sacrifice leading to the growth of the other person whom you love with commitment. This self-sacrifice results in an equal or even greater growth of our own self.

Again, I would like to share a poem by Kahlil Gibran from his book *The Prophet*. His words of wisdom about loneliness and separateness are important for a successful marriage.

> But let there be spaces in your togetherness,
> And let the winds of the heavens dance between you.
> Love one another, but make not a bond of love.
> Let it rather be a moving sea between the shores of your souls.
> Fill each other's cup, but drink not from one cup.
> Give one another of your bread, but eat not from the same loaf.
> Sing and dance together and be joyous, but let each one of you be alone,
> Even as the strings of the lute are alone though they quiver with the
> same music.
>
> Give your hearts but not into each other's keeping.
> For only the hand of Life can contain your hearts.
> And stand together yet not too near together:
> For the pillars of the temples stand apart,
> And the oak tree and the cypress grow not in each other's shadow.

This poem, which is full of wisdom, clearly shows the importance of individual growth in a marriage. A marriage is successful only when the uniqueness and individuality of the people involved are preserved, and the love and affection of these people induces each to have respect for the other's separateness. This has to be valued. Only then is there individual spiritual and mental growth of both involved in the marriage. This leads to a successful marriage and a happy married life.

As I mentioned, to have a happy marriage and a happy family, each of us has to respect the individuality of our spouse and our children. The two poems of Kahlil Gibran clearly indicate that we have to respect the individuality, uniqueness, and separateness of those we love. Only then can we have a happy married life.

In any marriage, there will be certain areas of disagreement and times of confrontation with our spouse and our children, and we have to exercise our own power with extreme humility. This can be done with an act of loving and caring confrontation rather than saying "I'm right, and you are wrong" or criticizing another right, left, and centre, shooting straight from the hip and not analyzing the whole situation properly. Quite commonly in marriages, one parent tries to exercise his or her power or superiority over the family because he or she is the main breadwinner. But, to have a happy marriage with happy children, one has to confront family members with extreme humility and love, especially when one has financial power. Sometimes we have to confront our children and show our leadership as parents. We have to have a judicious way of guiding our children when we think they are not on the right path. In many marriages, I see the criticisms and confrontations made with anger and annoyance. They are impulses, and they increase the amount of confusion in a family.

For a parent, the act of criticizing or confronting a child does not come easily. To such a parent, it is evident that it requires extreme humility and love to solve the child's problem—not angry confrontation but love and affection will show that you have intellectual superiority over your child and that you love that child. When you discipline children with genuine love, you recognize and respect the unique individuality and separateness of each and every person in the family. A genuinely loving person values the uniqueness and separateness of his or her spouse and children, and will be reluctant to always say, "I am right, and you are wrong."

In real life, we know that one person does often know better than another what is good because of his or her intellectual superiority or superior knowledge or wisdom in regards to the matter at hand. Under these circumstances, the wiser of the two usually has an obligation, which grows out of genuine love and concern for the mental and spiritual growth of the person being confronted, to guide the other person on the right path. A genuinely loving person, therefore, is frequently in a dilemma when caught between his or her loving respect others and his or her special skill or knowledge regarding the question over which there is confrontation. But, after extreme self-analysis and examination of the problem, one has to make a very responsible decision to guide the other member of the family on the right path with loving leadership, as is required in any confrontational situation arising in a family. The dilemma is painstaking and requires intensive self-scrutiny in which the lover examines with extreme caution the work of his or her wisdom, the motives behind the need to assume the leadership role, and the possibility of showing the right path to the spouse or the child with whom there is a disagreement. This act of self-scrutiny shows that we have extreme humility and love for our family.

The words of a fourteenth century English spiritual teacher written in *The Cloud of Unknowing* go very well here: "Meekness or humility in itself is nothing else than a true knowing and feeling of man's self as he is. Any man who truly sees and feels himself as he is must surely be meek indeed."

There are two ways to confront or criticize another human being. One is with spontaneous certainty and the belief that you are right, so you confront another with arrogance, a method commonly seen in many families. This produces resentment in a relationship. The second way is to confront with extreme humility and love. This is certainly not common, and it requires a genuine extension of one's self and the recognition of the individuality, uniqueness, and separateness of the person being confronted. If you know that you have the experience, knowledge, and intellectual superiority and that you are right in a particular situation, then you must guide the other person and express yourself in a concerned way to aid in his or her mental and spiritual growth.

Loving parents must first examine themselves and their values and determine accurately that they know what is the best for their child. After having determined this, and given great thought to the child's character and behaviour and the capacity of the child to analyze the situation, they should then provide the child with love and affection in the form of suggestions, permissions or prohibitions, the creation of experiences, the organization of access to others' opinions, and tactful questioning to guide their child on the proper path. If parents want to be heard, then they must speak using language at the child's level of understanding. They have to show genuine love with extreme humility and extend themselves with love and commitment. As parents, we want the inner mental and spiritual growth of our children.

1. Abraham Maslow, *Religions, Values and Peak Experiences* (New York: Viking, 1970).
2. Matthew 18:3 (King James)
3. Rollo May, *Love and Will* (New York: W.W. Norton, 1969), 220.
4. Joseph Goldstein, *Beyond the Best Interests of the Child* (New York: Free Press, 1973).
5. Kahlil Gibran, *The Prophet* (Ware, Hertfordshire: Wordsworth Editions, 1997), 8.
6. Kahlil Gibran, *The Prophet* (New York: Alfred Knopf, 1955), 15–16.
7. *The Cloud of Unknowing* (New York: Julian Press, 1969), 92.

CHAPTER 2

Laugh and Live in the Moment

Happiness means that we are very aware of the fact that we are glad and content with our lives and that we are enjoying ourselves. Seeking happiness is the very purpose of life. Happiness can be achieved by training our mind to bring about certain disciplines. With that, we can undergo a better transformation of our attitude and outlook towards life. This personal happiness can be manifested as a simple willingness to reach out to others and create a feeling of affinity and goodwill, even in the briefest of our encounters.

I remain quite impressed by the poetry of Kahlil Gibran from the book *Tears and Laughter*—especially by his reflections on emotions. If we are willing to trust our emotions knowing that, even though we do not understand them at the moment, each and every one of our experiences are there to support our positive thinking, to make a positive change, then we will immediately stop worrying. Instead, we will feel ourselves moving towards simple solutions, which lead to happiness, and, by making an emotion less intense, we cultivate feelings of appreciation for each emotion, whether it is laughter or tears in a positive sense. As the child that needs attention, we will find our emotions, when noticed, will, in fact, have a calming effect on us.

The poetry of Kahlil portrays this very well.

> I would not exchange the laughter of my heart for the fortunes of the multitudes;
> Nor would I be content with converting my tears, invited by my agonized self, into calm.
> It is my fervent hope that my whole life on this earth will ever be tears and laughter.

Tears that purify my heart and reveal to me the secret of life and its
mystery

Laughter that brings me closer to my fellow men;
Tears with which I join the broken-hearted,
Laughter that symbolizes joy over my very existence.
I prefer death through happiness a thousand fold to life in vain and in
despair.

An eternal hunger for love and beauty is my desire;
I know now that those who possess bounty alone are naught but
miserable,
But to my spirit the sighs of lovers
Are more soothing than music of the lyre.

When night comes, the flower folds its petals and slumbers with Love,
And at dawn, it opens its lips to receive the Sun's kisses,
Bespeckled by quick darting of clouds which come, but surely go.
The life of flowers is hope and fulfilment and peace, tears and laughter.

The water disappears and ascends until it turns into clouds that gather
upon the hills and valleys;
And when it meets the breeze, it falls down upon the fields and joins
the brook that sings its way toward the sea.
The life of clouds is a life of farewell and a life of reunion
Tears and laughter.

Thus the spirit separates itself from the body and walks into the world
of substance,
Passing like clouds over the valleys of sorrow and mountains of
happiness
Until it meets the breeze of death and returns to its starting place,
The endless ocean of love and beauty which is God.

Kahlil Gibran[1]

The above-quoted words of the great poet Kahlil Gibran, written about the ways of joy, are optimistic. Mystic poet, dramatist, and artist, Kahlil Gibran lived in the United States after 1910.

There is no other sound sweeter than the sound of laughter because it brings inner joy and happiness, as Dr. Deepak Chopra tells his audience. "The happy thoughts produce happy molecules, and tears of laughter produce different chemicals than the tears of sadness."

There is something about laughter that is extremely healing. As satirist Voltaire said, "In laughter, there is always a kind of joyfulness that is incompatible with contempt or indignation." Here Voltaire reminds us of the value of the sound of laughter, saying that it is virtually impossible to be sad or contemptuous and to laugh at the same time.

There is a true story about Norman Cousins in the book called *Anatomy of An Illness*. Cousins suffered an incurable illness that caused deterioration of his spinal cord and would eventually claim his life. He decided to have hilarious movies brought to his hospital room so that he could watch them every day. The comedians he watched included The Three Stooges, Abbot and Costello, and Jack Benny. This therapy was pure laughter. Cousins's book was a bestseller that described how he was cured of his terminal illness through the medicine of laughter.

When we laugh, we produce neuropeptides, which are endorphins. These cause relaxation of muscles, decrease the blood pressure, and produce an enormous healing impact on the body. It is fascinating that the tears of laughter have a different chemical makeup than the tears of sadness, as mentioned by Dr. Deepak Chopra.

A child's laughter is so sweet and has both tranquilizing and stimulant effects as it produces endorphins in our brain, which cause an extremely sweet effect in our bodies. When we listen to a child's laughter, our instincts tell us that we need to laugh to make life fun, to let ourselves shun bad thoughts, which have a hardening effect on our attitudes. It is not just the sounds of laughter but also the sounds of the trees, the birds, the winds, the sound of a waterfall and the rain—they are all so natural that we should listen to them and get deeper into our inner selves so that we can feel inner joy and happiness.

When my son Imran was very young, he had the most glorious laugh. Even now, when he laughs, he laughs with his full heart. That brings joy and happiness into our family. The way to cultivate the habit of laughter and a healthy sense of humour is to get with the child that resides in each one of us, regardless of our age. We have a tendency to equate growing up with becoming more serious. We believe maturity involves stiffening up. I believe in full-hearted laughter, which is like a child's laughter. This can bring a deeper joy and happiness.

I particularly like those who laugh at themselves rather than making fun of others. Sometimes I think of the things I have done—some of them are probably quite silly at times—and I laugh at myself. I have loved my teachers, and I have the most reverence for them. Those teachers with a wonderful sense of humour are most memorable. They were the ones who were not afraid to bring humour to the classroom, to teach dry subjects like anatomy or biochemistry or physics with a sense of humour. It made these subjects so easy to learn. The people I enjoy the most are those who have been around me who can laugh frequently and can provoke the same reaction in me, making me laugh with a child's laughter. All of my children fit this description—when they laugh, they laugh full heartedly. I see their faces light up with joy. I am always thrilled to see them laugh. In fact, just sitting here, imagining their laughter makes me feel happy and joyous. I encourage you to contemplate joy—even thinking about laughter can have a very therapeutic effect on the mind and body.

To put the wisdom of this poem by Kahlil Gibran into your life, I suggest that you spend some time with children, interacting with them, and see how frequently they laugh as they play.

Then, remind yourself that there is a child within you who has the same feelings. Be childlike, as said by Jesus of Nazareth, and allow yourself less control of your life. Allow the inner child in yourself to express itself in all the fun ways of life.

If you have labelled yourself as a serious person who does not have a sense of humour, then I suggest you change that label right now—learn to laugh like a child. You do not have to stick to that label anymore. Why remain a serious person simply because you have become one by habit? I suggest you make a conscious effort to laugh more often. Do not let a day go by without laughing. It is particularly important to laugh—especially on bad days. Remember Norman Cousins who was inflicted with a chronic disease. He basically cured his illness with the therapeutic effects of laughter.

You may have to be a little crazy at times and lighten up. Be childlike. Keep repeating this valuable lesson in your life to lighten up and be happy and joyous.

Why is it, when I am in Rome,
I would give an eye to be at home.
But, when on native earth I be,
My soul is sick for Italy?

And why with you, my love, my lord,
Am I spectacularly bored,
Yet, do you up and leave me–then
I scream to have you back again?
Dorothy Parker[4]

Dorothy Parker (1893–1967) was an American writer of short stories and poems, and she was noted for her wit. This poem is witty and clever, but it also carries an important message. Why is it that we don't enjoy the present moment and persistently neglect the present in favour of the past or future? Many of us suffer from this malady of not being fully immersed in the present moment. We are always living in the past or the future, yet the present is the only place in which we should fully immerse ourselves to be happy. Why do we use up the present moments of our lives and consume ourselves with past worries or fear of the unknown? Why do we use our present moments to be apprehensive about the future or to plan escapes to elsewhere? Dorothy Parker asks similar questions in her short poem.

I think the answer to these questions—about always living our lives either in the past or in the future and not in the present moment—is that we must consciously bring our attention to the present moment in order to live our lives with appreciation. If you find yourself in Rome, and you are thinking about being at home, give yourself a nudge and tell yourself to attend to the present moment rather than live in the past or future. This kind of self-talk will rescue us from the trap of not living life; it will bring our full attention to the present moment and allow us to be happy.

I have seen that highly functioning people have a great ability to shut off the past or future and live in the present moment. When you talk to these highly functioning, enlightened people, you have their full attention. When they speak to you, they look directly into your eye and give their full consideration. When you ask these people how they do that, their response is that there is no point in worrying about things over which one has no control. Second, it makes no sense to worry about those things over which one does have full control because this control means personal power.

The message is very important. We should repeat this again and again to ourselves, to learn from these evolved and highly functioning people.

In my experience as a physician, it is very important to give my full attention to the present moment, listening to the complaints of a patient, for example, and helping that patient in whatever way possible. If my attention is scattered or directed to the past or the future, or even if I am thinking about other sick patients who are in the hospital or in ICU, then I may not have my full attention, at that moment, with that particular patient, with the person's complaint. I may not be able to help that patient to the full extent expected of me, as a physician.

Therefore, it is very important that we have our full attention in the present moment; it is the secret to being happy and content with our lives. Henry

David Thoreau's advice about living in the present is as relevant today as it was in 1862:

> Above all, we cannot afford not to live in the present. He is blessed over all mortals who loses no moment of the passing life in remembering the past.[5]

There is always a past, but present is the present moment, which is a gift to us. Therefore, we should fully immerse ourselves in the present moment to be happy.

> Behold I show you a mystery. We shall not all sleep, but we shall all be changed, in a moment, in the twinkling of an eye.
> 1 Corinthians: 15:51

Living life in the present moment is essentially putting less attention on the worries, concerns, regrets, and mistakes that bother you. Stay in the present. It simply means living life now, with your attention fully engaged in the present moment, and not allowing your mind to carry you away to experiences removed from this moment. When you manage to do this, you not only enjoy the moment you are experiencing to the fullest extent possible, but you also bring out the best in your performance and creativity because you are far less distracted by wants, needs, concerns, past worries and regrets, and previous mistakes.

> There can be no transforming of darkness into light and of apathy into movement without emotion.
> *Carl Jung* [6]

You will probably see happy people around who always look content and seem to be smiling all the time, no matter what. These are the people who are living in the present moment of happiness. When you are bothered or upset, it is usually over something that has already happened or about something that has yet to be. Happy people know that—regardless of what happened yesterday, last month, or last year or what might happen later today, tomorrow, or next year—"now" is the only place where happiness can actually be found or experienced. Obviously, this doesn't mean that you are not affected by or don't learn from your past, or that you don't plan your future. It simply means that you understand that you are more effective, powerful, and positive with the energy of today, the energy of right now.

Children intuitively understand that life is a series of present moments, each moment to be experienced only once in full—one right after the other—if each one is to be important. They immerse themselves in the present and offer their full attention to the person they are with. I remember my daughter Nazeen, who was crying because she did not want to let my wife and I go out one evening when she was very young. She wanted our full attention. We called the babysitter, and, although she liked the babysitter, Nazeen was still crying for us not to go out for the evening. Somehow we managed to leave. I went out and looked through the window, and I saw that, within a few minutes, she had settled down and started playing with the babysitter. This made me think that she was living in a moment of happiness. Initially, she wanted our attention, but, when our attention was gone, she had the attention of the babysitter, and she was all smiles and laughter again, playing with the babysitter. This little episode tells us that we should be more like children who experience moment-to-moment happiness. They usually live in the present.

As we grow older, we develop worries and concerns. We have regrets. We have made some mistakes. We either live in the past or the future. But, if we think that moment-to-moment happiness is the way to go, and we do our best to live for the moment, then we are happy. As you take this strategy to heart, you will discover that being able to immerse yourself in the present moment is a worthwhile quality to develop, and, by doing so, you will gain the capacity to experience ordinary events in an extraordinary fashion.

You will spend far less time being bothered by life while spending more time enjoying life. You will spend less energy convincing yourself that "the past is history, the future is mystery, and the present moment is a gift to you." We all live in the present moment, and this moment will never be repeated in the next moment. So live in the moment to be truly happy inside. This is called moment-to-moment happiness, and I believe in it. I want you to live in this fashion of moment-to-moment happiness to be happy.

Can we achieve happiness by cultivating a self-centred nature? Not necessarily. In fact, survey after survey has shown that it is unhappy people who tend to be more self-focused; they are often socially withdrawn and even antagonistic. Happy people, in contrast, are generally found to be more sociable, flexible, and creative, and they are able to tolerate life's daily frustrations more easily. Most important, they are found to be more loving and forgiving than unhappy people are.

Research has also shown that happy people accept a certain quality of openness and willingness to reach out and help others. Still, we begin with the basic premise that the purpose of our life is to seek happiness. And this need not be a self-centred or selfish quest. The vision of happiness is a real objective—one that we can take positive steps towards achieving. We identify the factors that lead to a happier life—service to others included—and we search for happiness, which benefits not only ourselves but also our family and society at large.

> Ask and ye shall receive. Seek and you will find. Knock, and it will be opened to you.
> Matthew 7:7

Happiness is determined more by one's state of mind than by external events. Success may result in a temporary feeling of elation, or tragedy may send us into a period of depression, but, sooner or later, our overall level of happiness tends to migrate back to certain baselines. Psychologists call this process "adaptation," and we can see how this principle operates in our daily lives. Recognition from our peers may lift our mood for a while, but, sooner or later, it is customary for our emotions to level off. For example, a fallout with a friend over simple matters may produce a foul mood, but, within a matter of time, our spirits can rebound back to a normal functioning level.

Examples are lottery winners—their initial responses are within a range from extreme happiness to relief, but gradually emotions levels off. Studies have also demonstrated that people struck with cancer, blindness, or paralysis may recover to normal or near-normal levels of day-to-day happiness after an appropriate adjustment period or time. Some researchers have recently argued that individuals have characteristic levels of happiness or well-being that are genetically determined, at least to some degree. For example, a study of identical twins who shared the same genetic makeup found that they also tended to have very similar levels of well-being, regardless of whether they were raised together or apart.

This research has led some investigators to postulate a biological set point of happiness wired into our brains at birth. Even if genetic makeup plays a role in happiness (and the verdict is still out on whether genetics plays a role), there is still general agreement among psychologists that, no matter what level of happiness we are endowed with by nature, there are steps we can take to work with the mind to enhance our feelings of happiness. This is because our outlook largely determines moment-to-moment happiness. In fact, whether we are feeling happy or unhappy at any given moment in time often has little to do with our absolute conditions; rather, it is the function of how we perceive our situation—of how satisfied we are within ourselves.

Thoughts To Remember

Here are some important quotations to keep in mind:

> There are moments in life when you miss someone so much that you just want to pick them from your dreams and hug them for real! [But fortunately,] when the door of happiness closes, another opens; but often times we look so long at the closed door that we don't see the one which has been opened for us. Don't go for looks; they can deceive. Don't go for wealth; even that fades away. Go for someone who makes you smile because it takes only a smile to make a dark day seem bright. Find the one that makes your heart smile. Dream what you want to dream. Go where you want to go. Be what you want to be because you have only one life and one chance to do all the things you want to do. May you have enough happiness to make you sweet, enough trials to make you strong, enough sorrow to keep you humble, enough hope to make you happy.
>
> The happiest of people don't necessarily have the best of everything; they just make the most of everything that comes along their way.
>
> The brightest future will always be based on a forgotten past. You can't go forward in life until you let go of your past failures and heartaches.
>
> When you were born, you were crying and everyone around you was smiling. Live your life so, at the end, you're the one who is smiling and everyone around you is crying.[7]
>
> Life is not measured by the number of breaths we take, but by the moments that take our breath away.[8]
>
> Someday I'll be happy …
>
> We convince ourselves that life will be better after we get married, have a baby, then another.
>
> Then we are frustrated that the kids aren't old enough— we'll be more content when they are.
>
> After that, we're frustrated that we have teenagers to deal with. We will certainly be happy when they are out of that stage. We tell

ourselves that our life will be complete when our spouse gets his or her act together, when we get a nicer car, are able to go on a nice vacation, when we retire....

The truth is, there is no better time to be happy than right now. If not now, when? Your life will always be filled with challenges. It's best to admit this to yourself and decide to be happy anyway....

Happiness *is* the way.[9]

So, treasure every moment that you have and treasure it more because you shared it with someone special, special enough to spend your time with....

And remember... time waits for no one.

So, stop waiting... until your car or home is paid off. Until you get a new car or home. Until your kids leave home. Until you go back to school. Until you finish school. Until you lose 10 pounds. Until you gain 10 pounds. Until you get married. Until you get a divorce. Until you have kids. Until you retire. Until summer. Until spring. Until winter. Until fall.... Until you die.

There is no better time than right now to be happy. Happiness is a journey, not a destination.[10]

So, as the adage goes, "work like you don't need money, love like you've never been hurt, and dance like no one's watching."

---

1. Kahlil Gibran, *Tears and Laughter*, (New York, Citadel Press, 1949), 13.
2. For more on this see Deepak Chopra, *Creating Health: How to Wake up the Body's Intelligence* (Boston, Houghton Mifflin, 1995), p. 82
3. John Templeton, *Wisdom from World Religions: Pathways Toward Heaven on Earth* (Philadelphia: Templeton Foundation Press, 2002), 236.
4. Dorothy Parker, *The Portable Dorothy Parker* (Harmondsworth: Penguin Books, 1976), 227.
5. Henry David Thoreau, *"Walking," The Atlantic Monthly*, June 1862, 673.
6. Carl G. Jung, *Psychological Reflection: An Anthology of the Writings of Carl G. Jung* (New York: Harper, 1961), 32.
7. Greg S. Kessler, ed., *Internet Wisdom: The Best of Internet E-Mail Wit and Wisdom* (Bloomington, IN: AuthorHouse, 2007), 82.
8. George Carlin, quoted in *The Real Meaning of Life*, ed. David Seaman (Novato, CA: New World Library, 2005), 69.
9. Richard Carlson, *Don't Sweat the Small Stuff* (New York: Hyperion, 1997), 169.
10. *Angel Whisperer's Blog*, vol. 1, comp. Kelli Jansen (Toronto: Lulu, 2008), 97.

CHAPTER 3

Pain and Suffering

The first of the four greatest truths – life is suffering.
Buddha

One of the greatest truths is that life is full of difficulties and suffering. It is a great truth once we truly see this truth. We try to understand and accept it. Once we truly know that life is difficult, then it is no longer difficult because, once we accept this fact about life, suffering becomes natural, a part of the fabric of life. We accept life's struggles as truth. Once we know that life is difficult, then we will try to learn how to accept life and not moan about it. Then we try to solve the problems and discipline ourselves, as discipline is the basic tool that is required to solve life's problems. It is very difficult to solve anything without discipline. Only with discipline can we solve a problem. With total discipline, we could probably solve all the problems of our life.

Solving the problems is painful. Problems, depending upon their nature, evoke frustration, grief, sadness, loneliness, guilt, anger, regret, fear, anxiety, despair, or anguish. These are very uncomfortable feelings. They can produce physical pain. Because the pain leads to conflict, this poses an endless series of problems, and life seems always difficult, full of pain and suffering. We cannot see the other side of life, which is the true joy we can reach if we have the discipline in our mind to accept and solve our problems.

> Those things that hurt, instruct.
> *Benjamin Franklin*[1]

Problems definitely hurt, yet it is the whole process of meeting and solving the problems that makes our lives quite meaningful. Problems are a cutting edge that distinguishes between failure and success. They call forth our courage and wisdom. It is only because of the problems that we grow spiritually and mentally. When we encourage the growth of our inner spirit, then we challenge and encourage the human capacity to solve these problems. It is comforting to know that pain and suffering bring out the best in us and encourage us to grow both mentally and spiritually. It is very well said by Benjamin Franklin that those things that hurt always instruct. Therefore, the wise people learn to learn from problems and not to dread but to actually welcome them. They grow spiritually when they solve these problems.

Problems are always involved with pain, and, fearing the pain involves us, to a greater or lesser extent, in trying to avoid these problems, in trying to procrastinate, so they will go away. We also ignore problems and pretend that they never existed. This act of evasion happens when people go on drugs—they attempt to prevent the pain and skirt problems rather than meet them head on. We all attempt to get out of problems rather than suffer through them. We do not have the courage to face them, as most of us are not very wise.

> Neurosis is always a substitute for legitimate suffering.
> *Carl Jung*[2]

Emotional suffering is inherent in working through any problem. However, we seek to avoid pain by dismissing or ignoring the reality of our suffering. It is this disregard for the reality of our suffering that is the primary basis for all mental illness. Most of us have a tendency to go to extraordinary lengths to avoid problems and suffering, as both cause pain. We will go as far as taking the easy way out rather than accepting the problem. We will go to elaborate lengths to have fantasies in which to live, in a comfort zone, rather than suffering through the problems. Total exclusion of reality leads to neuroses. As Carl Jung explains so well, "neurosis is always a substitute for legitimate suffering."

When we try to avoid legitimate suffering, we basically avoid our mental and spiritual growth. The substitute, our neurosis, excels; our problems become more painful, and we substitute even more neurotic behaviour. It is true that many of us fall into this trap of feeding neurosis by avoiding suffering and not facing it head on, which leads to acute-on-chronic neurosis, leading to acute-on-chronic mental illness. This avoidance of suffering basically leads us to stop growing mentally and spiritually, and we get stuck, usually in the first or second phase of our mental growth. We usually shrivel our spirit, and, without healing, we languish intellectually and never achieve wisdom.

Therefore, we should teach our children and ourselves how to grow mentally and spiritually: by suffering through problems and by disciplining ourselves and facing problems head on. It becomes very clear that these tools and techniques of suffering mean that we are experiencing the pain of the problem in such a way that we have to work through the problems and solve them successfully, which will lead to inner growth. The tools and techniques of suffering allow us to experience the pain of the problem constructively by having a different mindset. The disciplined mind is the one that will deal head on with these problems.

There are four ways of dealing with legitimate suffering and with the problems that are inherent in our lives. These four ways are

1. delaying gratification
2. accepting responsibility
3. dedicating ourselves to truth
4. living a balanced life

Actually, these are very simple tools. We can learn to adopt them easily. Children from age 10 and up can quickly learn these four responsibilities of life, which will enable them to have satisfactory mental and spiritual growth. We do see the disciplined mind emerging from following these four ways, which, as I mentioned, we should teach ourselves and our children in order to achieve mental and emotional growth. Yet, we see the kings and presidents forget to use these tools, and they have their downfalls because they have not grown spiritually or mentally. The complexity of these tools is basically that the pain has to be confronted rather than avoided. If one seeks to avoid legitimate suffering, then one will avoid the use of these tools of discipline: that is, delaying gratification, accepting responsibility, dedicating ourselves to truth, and leading a balanced life. If we do not have this discipline in life, then we are stuck in the first or second phase of our mental growth and will never get out of it. We see this kind of attitude in all circles of people—the rich, the poor, the most educated, or the uneducated. It suggests that we have to become aware that pain and suffering are a part of life, and we have to accept this and deal with it head on with disciplined action. As I mentioned, this action means using the tools of delaying gratification to experience the problem, accepting responsibility for the problem, leading a balanced life while suffering through the problem, and dedicating ourselves to discovering the truth about the problem and its true solution. That is the only way we can grow mentally and spiritually.

Life is suffering. The only way we can come out of suffering is to have a disciplined mind.

To repeat, we should face the problems in life head on by

1. delaying gratification
2. accepting responsibility
3. dedicating ourselves to truth (The truth shall set you free)
4. living a balanced life

1. Delaying Gratification

I was referred a 50-year-old homecare nurse by a family physician to assess her for chest pain. I did routine cardiac stress testing, an echocardiogram and Holter monitor. All of these tests came back normal. I reported back to the family physician that she did not have any cardiac disease significant enough to cause her chest pain. She had a history of hypertension, which was under good control. This lady had presented to the Emergency Department on a few occasions with chest pains. Her routine electrocardiograms and cardiac enzymes were normal, so she would be sent home after having been told she had atypical chest pains or chest wall pain—or just pains due to underlying stress and anxiety. The family physician referred her back to me, and, after a few months, I again had to do one more stress test—a nuclear medicine study called a Thallium stress test or MIBI or myocardial perfusion study—to make sure she truly did not have underlying coronary artery disease. Her Thallium study (MIBI) was perfectly normal. Again, I reassured her there was a 90 to 95 per cent chance that she did not have coronary artery disease to cause her atypical chest pains.

She presented again to the Emergency Department on two more occasions, and was referred back to me again by the emergency physician. This time, the idea was to send her for a coronary angiography, which is the standard test these days to say that truly the chest pains are not due to coronary artery disease. I reviewed her again, and, as usual, I went into the depth of the problem. Seeing that her chest pains were atypical and all of her tests were normal, I wondered whether her chest pains were psychological in nature. I started to delve into the psychological analysis for chest pain, and, when I questioned her, asking her about her social life, family life, and workplace, she began to procrastinate about her work, saying it was quite difficult and she did not enjoy it anymore. Her supervisor would be forceful to her. She was a homecare nurse, and she would make house calls, looking after sick patients in their homes. I asked her how she started her day. She replied that she would first go to see the patients who were stable and easy, who would not require any major assistance. They would require simple tasks, which would not be stressful. Then, by the afternoon or towards the end of her day, she would see the very sick patients or the tough patients. She would not complete her work and would get frustrated. These homecare nurses must see a certain number of patients in a day, and she was leaving all of the difficult patients who required a lot of nursing care to the end of her day. She would definitely get frustrated, and she was being reprimanded by her supervisor.

I suggested to her that it would be better to see her very sick and difficult patients early in the mornings and leave the easier patients for the end of the day; then, her life would probably become easier. She did follow my advice, and noted that she was able to finish her work schedule in time. Her supervisor, also, was happier with her work.

The point here is that gratification should be delayed, so life can really be enjoyed. Delaying gratification is a very important aspect in life so that we can enjoy life. This concept has been mentioned in many psychology books, but I have noted myself that, whenever I make my hospital rounds, I will do all of the critical care or the sickest patients first, and then I will go to the ward to see those less critical. So, by the time I arrive at my office, I have taken care of all of the sick patients who require more of my attention and are more stressful. Then, I have less stress for my office patients, which are more stable and elective consultations. It is very important that we delay gratification. If we do that, then our mind is more relaxed and at rest so that we can enjoy our work.

When I was getting into the psychological aspect of this nurse's chest pain, I delved a little deeper into her history, asking about such things as her childhood, to see why she was behaving the way she was at work. I found out that she had had a difficult childhood. Her parents separated when she was very young, and she did not get a lot of love and attention, which are required in early childhood.

Delaying gratification is actually a process of scheduling the pain and pleasure of life in such a way that we enhance the pleasure by meeting and experiencing the pain first and getting over it. Then, we will have enough time in our day to enjoy pleasures. This process of scheduling is learned by children quite early in life, sometimes as early as age five. I remember I was in a Catholic school in India, and the toughest periods of education, such as mathematics or the sciences, would be early in the mornings. Later in the day, we would have easier courses. At the end of the day, we would have the physical activities, such as games. That has taught me that delaying gratification is very important and should be taught very early in our childhood education. By the age of twelve, some children are already able to understand this very well, and, with proper parenting, they are able to complete their homework as soon as they get home, before watching television or playing games. By the age of fifteen or sixteen, such behaviour is definitely expected in adolescents who are considered to be normal.

It becomes very clear from this that educators have to learn that a substantial number of adolescents who fall into this norm have to have the tough part of their education done in the early mornings and the fun part of education and life delayed until later in the day.

While many have developed the capacity to delay gratification, there are also those adolescents who have not developed this capacity at all. They are problem students, even though they may have average or better intelligence. Their grades are usually poor. These are the adolescents who skip classes and are very impulsive, and that spills into their social life as well. They may get into frequent fights or get into alcohol and drugs. Also, they may have confrontations with other students, family, or authority figures like the police. Some psychologists and psychotherapists are called in at this stage of their lives, but it usually too late by then.

These adolescents are quite resentful, and impulsive, and, often, their problems go so deep that participation in psychotherapy becomes meaningless to them. They begin to miss their appointments, and they will avoid important and painful issues, which would be, in fact, helpful to them if they would let them be discussed with psychotherapists or psychologists. The attempts at intervention fail, and these children drop out of school. Not only do they have a pattern of failure, they frequently end up in disastrous marriages, in an accident, in a psychiatric hospital, or even in jail.

Why is it that the majority of children develop the capacity to delay gratification while a very substantial number fail to develop this capacity? The answer to this is not absolutely clear, or scientifically proven. The role of genetics is also very unclear at this time. The variables cannot be sufficiently controlled by any scientific proof. Therefore, the signs point to the quality of parenting as a determinant in the early part of childhood.

The children who are undisciplined, or lacking in parental discipline of any sort, are the children who are punished frequently and severely throughout childhood. These are the children who are punched, kicked, slapped, beaten, or even whipped by their parents, even for a minor infraction of family rules. In fact, this form of child rearing is what I call very undisciplined discipline. When parents try to teach their children in this way, it is truly meaningless.

The reason it is meaningless is that the parents, themselves, are undisciplined, and they therefore serve as a bad "model" of being lacking in discipline. They are the ones who say, "Do as I say, and not as I do." They frequently get into fights with each other, or they may get drunk in front of their children. They are the ones who do not have any restraints or dignity or rationality within themselves. They are the ones who don't keep any promises. These are the parents who frequently have their own lives in despair and disorder.

When we are young, we look, with our child-like eyes, up to our parents as God-like figures. But when parents do things their own way and do not understand and treat their children as childish, rather than as responsible for every little mistake, when parents, at the same time, do not have any self-discipline, restraint, or dignity, or the capacity to have order in their own lives, then children will come to feel, in the deepest part of themselves, that this lack of self-discipline is the way to live a normal life. Children who see their parents' pain day in and day out and who experience their parents acting without any self-discipline, will go out into the world with deep desires to be just like their parents. They will begin to believe that it is the way life should be lived.

The most important thing for a parent is to be a role model for love. Even in the chaotic disorder of homes, genuine love is present. From such homes may come self-disciplined children. Infrequently, parents who are professionals—for example, doctors, lawyers and teachers—and who lead lives of strict orderliness but yet lack love, send children into the world who are as undisciplined, destructive, and disorganized as any child from an undisciplined family or a chaotic home.

Therefore, I think love is everything. The mystery of love will bring ultimate peace to the family network. When we love something, then we spend a lot of time with that entity and value it. For instance, a teenager who loves his car spends time admiring it, polishing it, repairing it, and tuning it up. A mother who loves her garden will spend time pruning, mulching, and fertilizing it. Therefore, when we love our children, we spend time admiring them, caring for them, and giving time to them. That brings about good discipline in them. Good discipline definitely requires time full of love. When we have no time to give to our children, or no time that we are willing to give, then we become aware of their misdeeds too late to give loving guidance. In other words, we discover our children's misdeeds or bad behaviour too late when we are unwilling to give quality time to our offspring. This causes irritation. Then we say things like, "I just don't have the energy to deal with it."

Finally, when the misdeeds become an irritation, then we start to impose discipline in a cruel way, without examining the problem or even taking the time to consider which form of discipline would be most appropriate to that particular problem.

The parents who love their children and devote time to their children are the ones who discipline their children in a positive way: by way of praise when they do good things and telling them little stories or giving them little lectures in an appropriate manner, with kisses and hugs now and then. This leads to a positive energy flowing from the parents to their children.

Therefore, it is the quality of discipline that matters. It is superior to the love given by the unloving parents. It is very important to take the time to observe and think about our children's needs. Loving parents will frequently suffer when their children suffer. The children are not blind to this, and they perceive when their parents are willing to suffer when they are suffering. They may not respond with immediate gratitude at that time, but, when they see that their parents are willing to suffer with them when they are suffering, then they will tell themselves that the suffering must not be so bad, and, therefore, they should be willing to suffer with the parents. This is the beginning of the self-discipline that is noted in loving families.

The children from loving families feel that they are valuable. This feeling is very essential to good mental health. It is the cornerstone of self-discipline. It is the by-product of loving parenthood. Such a belief or conviction must be gained in childhood. It is extremely difficult to acquire this self-esteem in adulthood. Conversely, when children have learned, through the love of their parents, to feel valuable, it is not possible for them in adulthood to destroy their spirit of love.

The great feeling of valuable love is the cornerstone of self-discipline because, when one considers one's self as very valuable, then one will take care of one's self in every way possible. Self-discipline is called "self-caring." In relation to the process of delaying gratification, caring about self is important; when we feel ourselves to be valuable and worthy of care, then we know that our time is also valuable—and we want it to be used in a significant and valuable way—so we are willing to pass up transient and immediate pleasures to pursue meaningful projects that give us lasting joy.

As in the case of our homecare nurse who procrastinated in her job and was not happy, the unhappiness was rooted deep in her self and arose from her unhappy childhood; she was brought up in a dysfunctional family, as her parents did not want to take care of her while she was growing up. Therefore, she was feeling herself to be of little value, not worth caring for. Therefore, she did not care for herself. She did not feel it was worth disciplining herself, despite the fact that she was a very intelligent and competent nurse. She required the most elementary instruction in self-discipline because she lacked a realistic assessment of herself—of her own worth and the value of her own time.

The experience of parental love and caring throughout childhood will allow people to enter adulthood not only with a deep internal sense of their own value but also with a deep internal sense of security. A substantial number of children are actually not loved in dysfunctional families due to single parents, sheer negligence, a death in the family, financial problems, or a simple lack of caring by the parents. Some parents actually try to discipline their children by saying that they won't love them if they don't follow parental demands. These parents sacrifice love for the need for control and domination over the child. The result is that the children become fearful of the future. These children are psychologically insecure in their adulthood, lacking any deep sense that the world is safe and productive. To the contrary, they see the world as dangerous and frightening. They are not about to forfeit any gratification or security in the present for the promise of future gratification or security. For them, the future is very dubious, at best, and insecure indeed.

In summary, children who develop the capacity to delay gratification have loving and caring parents. If they do not develop this capacity during childhood, then they have an uphill struggle in adulthood. Often, this struggle is unsuccessful.

Problems in life usually don't just go away. We have to work through these problems. Otherwise they remain forever as a deterrent to inner mental and spiritual growth. The problems become more deep-seated and destructive because we have the tendency to be impatient. We make inadequate attempts to find instant solutions. This defect is quite universal. We always hope that the problems will go away on their own accord. We do not pay attention or give time to solve the problem. Remember homecare nurse; she continued to gratify herself by doing easy jobs in the mornings and leaving the more difficult patients to the later part of the day. Her work would never be done, and she would be frustrated as she was disciplined by her supervisor. When I pointed this out to her, she started thinking about it. She worked to correct this problem. But when I first discussed this idea with her, she was not aware of what she was doing wrong, and she thought her supervisor would probably quiet down and not be too picky about it. She thought the problem would go away on its own. Problems usually do not go away on their own; you need to work at them. We have to first analyze a problem and then deal with it head on.

The inclination to ignore problems is again a simple manifestation of not wanting to delay gratification. As I mentioned, confronting problems can be painful. But, when we are willing to confront a problem early, then we are forced to confront it by putting aside something pleasant or less painful for something more painful. It is better to suffer early in the hope of future gratification, which is more rewarding than choosing to continue to have present gratification in the hopes that future suffering will not be necessary.

In the case of the homecare nurse who ignored obvious problems, she was emotionally immature or psychologically primitive. But I think she is in every person. Her immaturity and primitiveness exist in most of us. These characteristics are quite common, even in big organizations. Corporate executives, who are recognized as mature people, sit looking at a problem, and think that it will go away on its own. They do not really tackle problems in time. These are the big corporations that usually collapse.

Parents, or executives, or many of us are ill prepared to tackle a task. Most parents do brush aside problems within their children or in their relationships with their children for months or years before they take any effective action. When you ask them, they usually respond that they thought their child would "grow out of it." When these parents bring their children to a psychiatrist, it is usually found that the problem may have started up to five years ago.

A word about the complexity of parenting: It must be said that parental decisions can be difficult, and children often do grow out of problems. But it never hurts to try to help them grow out of difficulties or to look more closely at the problem at hand and help them work through it. Never ignore the problem, relying on the fact that your child will grow out of it.

When children do not grow out of problems and tackling these problems is constantly postponed, the future can be bleak. The longer the children's problems are ignored, the larger these problems become, and the more painful and difficult they are to solve in later years.

2. Accepting Responsibility

Case Studies

STUDY NUMBER ONE

I was consulted on a 40-year-old man to assess him for progressive shortness of breath. On taking his history, I discovered that he was on disability from his company because of his shortness of breath. He admitted to drinking alcohol, maybe four or five drinks a day for a number of years. His cardiopulmonary investigations revealed that he had poor left ventricular function (Grade III) or congestive heart failure, with poor heart pump function as well. His angiograms were normal, and, therefore, he did not have any underlying coronary artery disease. The cause of his poor heart function was related to excessive alcohol intake. I made the diagnosis of alcoholic cardiomyopathy.

Then, I went a little deeper into his history. I questioned him: "Why do you drink so much alcohol?" And he stressed that he had nothing better to do. He was on disability, and he was bored sitting around at home. I suggested he take up a hobby, but his response was that he had no interest in any hobbies. He was divorced and single at the present time. Going much deeper into his psychological history, I felt that this man was blaming everyone else for his own actions. He had too many issues about his marriage and his previous wife, and also he was not happy with his job. He didn't take any blame for any of his actions, and he was blaming the circumstances for his problems.

This is a clear-cut case of character disorder, when a person does not take responsibility and blames others for his or her situation and circumstances.

STUDY NUMBER TWO

A 30-year-old lady was admitted to ICU for a drug overdose when I was taking critical care calls. We put her on life support, and, the next morning when she woke up, she realized she had made mistakes. I asked her why she took an overdose, and her answer was, obviously, that she wanted to die. On further questioning, I learned that she was blaming herself for everything—a broken relationship with her boyfriend, a not having a steady job.... During the whole interview, she was regretful but blaming herself for the circumstances she was in at the present time. I am not a psychiatrist, but I do try to take a psychological history so that I can help these patients if I can. Otherwise, I refer them to a psychiatrist. I felt this lady was taking the blame for everything and was suffering from a neurosis. Neurotics assume too much responsibility, and they are in conflict with the world as they automatically assume blame for all of the problems facing them.

These two individuals that I have described are two sides of the same coin—one with a character disorder who would not take any responsibility for his actions and would blame everything on the world and one with a neurosis who would assume all of the responsibility, always blaming herself and never anything else.

> If you are not part of the solution, then you are part of the problem.
> *Eldridge Cleaver*

We must accept responsibility for a problem before we can solve it. We cannot solve a problem by saying it is not *my* problem. We cannot solve a problem by hoping that someone else will solve it for us. I can solve a problem only when I say, "This is my problem, and it is up to me to solve it." Many of us seek to avoid the pain of the problem, or we say to ourselves that the problem was caused by other people or by social circumstances, both of which are beyond our control. Therefore, we claim, it is up to the society at large or to those we feel are responsible to solve our problem. It is not my personal problem.

The extent to which many of us go to avoid assuming responsibility for our own personal problems, while sad, is real. Many see a psychiatrist for neuroses or character disorders, which are very common. These two conditions or disorders are simply avoidance of dealing with problems and reality. As such, they are awkward styles of relating to the world and its challenges. Usually, the neurotic assumes too much responsibility and the person with a character disorder does not assume enough responsibility. When neurotics are in conflict with the world, they automatically assume they are at fault, whereas, when those with character disorders are in conflict with the world, they automatically assume that the world is at fault. The two are in contrast to each other.

The speech from neurotics is different from that from the people with character disorders. The speech of a neurotic is notable for expressions such as "I should" and "I shouldn't," indicating that the individual's self-image is inferior, that the person feels he or she always falls short of the mark and is always making the wrong choices. The speech of a person with a character disorder relies heavily on "I can't," "I couldn't," "I have to," and "I had to," which demonstrates the self-image of a being who has no power of choice. For this person, behavior is completely directed by external forces beyond his or her control. Neurotics are actually easy to work with in psychotherapy because they assume responsibility for their difficulties and therefore see themselves as having problems. But those with character disorders are much more difficult to work with because they don't see themselves as the source of their problems. They see the world rather than themselves as being in need of a change. Therefore, they fail to recognize the necessity for self-assessment. Many individuals have both neurotic and character disorder characteristics. Clinically, these people are referred to as "character neurotics," a term indicating that, in some areas of their lives, there is a guilt complex by virtue of having assumed too much responsibility that is not really theirs while, in other areas of their lives, they fail to take realistic responsibility for themselves. Fortunately, after a psychiatrist or psychologist has established the faith and trust of these individuals in the psychotherapy process, through helping them with the neurotic part of their personalities, it is often possible to engage them in examining and correcting their unwillingness to assume responsibility when and where it is appropriate.

Distinguishing what we are responsible for from what we are not responsible for in this life is one of the greatest problems of human existence. It is never completely solved during the entirety of our lives. We must continually assess and reassess where our responsibilities fall in the ever-changing course of our lives. The assessment and reassessment of ourselves is painless if we perform it adequately and conscientiously. In the process, to perform adequately, we must possess the willingness and capacity to suffer continual self-assessment. Such a capacity for or willingness to engage in self-assessment is not inherent in many of us. In children with character disorders, there is an instinctual tendency to deny responsibility in the conflicts in which they find themselves. When we see two siblings fighting, each will usually blame the other for initiating the fight. Each will deny that he or she may have been the culprit. On the other hand, some children have neuroses in that they will assume responsibility for certain deprivations that they may experience but yet do not understand. The child who is not loved by his parents will assume that he or she is unlovable, rather than seeing the parent as deficient in the capacity to love.

As we grow from childhood through adolescence to adulthood, we go through a vast number of experiences and a lengthy, successful maturation, so we gradually gain the capacity to see the world, and our place in it, in a realistic manner. Then we are able to assess our responsibility for our self and our place in this world.

Parents can assess their children in the maturation process. Many opportunities for this assessment come about while the children are growing up, and the parents can either confront them and guide them with love and affection or completely escape their own responsibility and take no action when it is required. We have to seize these opportunities when they arise. The parents' sensitivity to a child's need, and their willingness to take the time necessary to guide their child, may often result in uncomfortable efforts to meet these needs, but these efforts are rewarded. In turn, it requires love and willingness to assume appropriate responsibilities for further enhancement of the child's mental growth.

Neurotic parents, because of their general willingness to assume too much responsibility, may even be quite excellent parents if their neuroses are relatively mild and they are not so overwhelmed by unnecessary responsibilities that they have scant energy left for the necessary responsibilities of parenthood. On the other hand, parents with a character disorder make disastrous parents because they often disrespect their children with vicious remarks, leading to the destruction of the character of their children. It is said that "Neurotics make themselves miserable. Those with character disorders make everyone else miserable."

And parents with character disorders certainly make their own children miserable. As in other areas in their lives, they fail to assume adequate responsibility for their own parenting. They tend to brush off their children in many little ways when these young people actually need their attention. When their children have problems in school, these parents usually blame the school system or blame other children. Finally, in their effort to avoid responsibility for their own lives, character disorder parents will often lay this responsibility on their children by saying things like "Because of you, I could not pursue a career" or "Because of you, I stay married to your father who drives me nuts" or "Because of you, my whole life is ruined." Such statements lay blame on their children and help them avoid taking responsibility as a parent. Parents with character disorders lack the capacity to see how inappropriate this is. The children will often accept this responsibility, and these children have a tendency to become neurotic. So parents with character disorders almost invariably produce neurotic children, or children with character disorders.

People suffering from character disorders are ineffective and destructive. These are the same character traits that usually extend into their friendships, business dealings, and marriages—and to any area of their existence in which they fail to assume responsibility for their own actions. This failure inevitably leads to the problem that cannot be solved because the individual has not assumed responsibility for solving the problem. The individual with a character disorder blames everyone else for the problem, such as their spouse, child, friend, parent, or employer—everyone except themselves. By casting away their responsibility, they feel comfortable with themselves, but they fail to solve the problems of daily living. They have ceased to grow mentally and spiritually and become a heavy weight on society.

> If you could only love enough, you could be the most powerful person in the world.
> *Emmett Fox*[4]

As I have discussed, love is a great emotion. Deprivation of love during childhood leads to problems like neuroses, character disorders, and being unable to delay gratification.

The ability to love purely and freely in all of the so-called ways that make the passion of love come alive is a gift. The message to all of us is very clear: we should take our time to express love in every way possible—especially to our children as they are growing up. Convey your feelings as much as possible and also express love to all creations of nature. I believe that all creatures of this world and the creations of nature are manifestations of God.

My all-time favorite Biblical quotation on love is 1:13 Corinthians: "If I could speak all the languages of earth and of angels, but didn't love others, I would only be a noisy gong or a clanging cymbal." This is a beautiful quotation, which says we are nothing without love. It speaks of the kindness of love and the absence of boasting, rudeness, and self-seeking. It does not delight in evil and it rejoices with truth. It concludes with this great message: "And now these three remain: Faith, Hope, and Love. But the greatest of these is Love." It is very important that children, as they are growing up, have true unconditional love from their parents so that they do not have problems with anxiety disorders, neuroses, depression, character disorders, or an inability to delay gratification. These and many other psychiatric problems are not uncommon in adults who were not loved when they were very young, when they were in the developing phases of their mental growth.

How do we cultivate love? We should let go of our impulse to judge others. We should refuse to feel good about the mistakes and sufferings of others. We should live lessons of kindness rather than just read these lessons at our churches, temples, or mosques. We should not desire for revenge and replace this anger with forgiveness. We should choose to love whenever and wherever possible by simply making that choice. Love is a very positive energy, so powerful that it can literally hold together every person in this universe. It is like a glue that unites nature. As said very well by Robert Browning, "Take away love, and our earth is a tomb!"[5]

We know that, when the energy of love is absent, we can do our part to revive it by cultivating love full of compassion with no conditions attached. It is unconditional love.

We should put away thoughts of anger, judgment, revenge, and hatred by becoming aware of them when they surface in our day-to-day life. We should simply tell ourselves that we do not want to think that way—refuse to allow any negative thoughts or emotions to destroy our lives. When we are confronted by hateful gossip or mean-spiritedness, we should just respond with a position of love. We should say simply that we do not want to make any judgments of anyone. Rather than criticizing a mean-spirited person, we just silently use the ability to project love as people who are full of love for the creations of nature, which are manifestations of God.

Our essential nature is kind and compassionate; these traits are the predominant features of human nature. Anger, violence, and aggression may certainly arise from a secondary or more superficial level, and, when we are frustrated, when we don't achieve love and affection, there is definitely a tendency towards anger, violence, and aggression.

Looking at human evolution and comparing it to that of animals, we see that human intelligence has developed over a number of years. As the environment became more complex, there was a greater need for more intelligence and for the cognitive ability to meet the increasing demands of a more complex environment. Fundamentally, human nature is gentleness and, because of the emergence of a more complex environment, intelligence has gradually developed. Intelligence can develop in an unbalanced way if not counterbalanced with compassion and love. Then, it becomes destructive. It is very important to recognize that human conflict is created by the misuse of human intelligence. We can utilize our intelligence to find a means to overcome these conflicts. Human intelligence, when combined with goodness and knowledge, makes human actions constructive. We should combine a warm heart with knowledge and education, and, also, we should learn to respect others' views and rights. This, then, becomes the basis of our spirit of reconciliation that can be used to overcome aggression and to resolve conflict.

The Buddhist doctrine of Buddha's nature provides some grounds for the belief that the fundamental nature of all sentient beings is essentially gentle and not aggressive. This philosophy, by its very nature, refers to the underlying basic and gentle nature of human beings. The basic spirit of mind present in all human beings is completely untainted by negative emotions or thoughts. There are also grounds to believe that human affection or compassion is not just a religious matter but that we have inherited a gentle human nature. For example, when a baby is born, the mother has the desire to feed her baby milk, and this gentle instinct is inherited. As she continues to feed, there is more compassion and love, and the bond of togetherness in this relationship between a mother and her baby will gradually grow with time.

Our physical structure itself is suited for a feeling of love and compassion. We see the calming effects that these feelings hold, and the beneficial effects on our health and physical well-being. Conversely, a feeling of frustration, fear, agitation, or anger leads to destruction, as well as to poor physical and emotion health.

> Only those who have learned the power of sincere and selfless contribution experience this as life's deepest joy: true fulfillment.
> *Anthony Robbins*[6]

We know that, to seek happiness, we have to love. We should have the affection and closeness, the love and compassion for our children to bring true happiness to ourselves. To be happy, we should have a warm and compassionate state of mind. We all have the potential for compassion, as it is the basic impulse of human nature, which is a nature of gentleness. We are born with that gene, of gentleness. It is just that we have to cultivate compassion and altruism when we are dealing with people, especially our children as they are growing up. We have to express love in every way and form as they are growing up so that, when they reach adulthood, they do not develop mental health issues or mental illnesses, as I mentioned, such as anxiety, neuroses, depression, character disorders, and so on.

Dr. Hilde Bruch has written a book called *Learning Psychotherapy*. In it, she states that basically all patients come to see a psychiatrist for one basic problem—a sense of helplessness, the fear and inner conviction of being unable to cope and to change things. There is a sense of insecurity in the majority of patients who desire to partially or totally escape the pain of freedom. Therefore, their failures are related to not accepting responsibility for the problems in their lives. They feel insecure because they have, in fact, given the power of controlling their lives to someone or something other than themselves. If they want to be healed of the problem, sooner or later they have to accept responsibility for their own lives. The whole of adult life is a series of personal choices and decisions, and one has to accept totally the responsibility of these choices and decisions. One has to become a free person. The desire to escape from freedom is very common, and, in a book written by Erich Fromm, aptly titled *Escape from Freedom* (known in Britain as *The Fear of Freedom*), he talks about this escape from freedom as a desire to avoid the pain of responsibility. He claims that millions or even billions of people daily attempt to escape from freedom. By this, he means that people just give away their power—to an entity called fate or to society, the government, a corporation, or a boss—that they do not accept any responsibility for their actions. Basically, we are trying to escape from freedom. When we give away this responsibility to someone else, then we are definitely ruled by others to whom we have given this responsibility. The point here is that we have to accept our responsibility, and we should not escape from the freedom of this responsibility, which is given to us as free people. We should not escape but rather accept the responsibility as free people and take responsibility for our actions.

3. *Dedicating Ourselves to Truth*

> And the truth shall set you free.
> John 8:32

The first tool of discipline in problem solving is dedication to truth. If we want a healthy attitude towards life, if we want our spirit to grow, then we should have a dedication to truth. Always, truth is reality. Anything that is false is unreal. The clearer we see the reality of the world, the better equipped we are to deal with problems in this world. The less clearly we see the truth or reality of the world, the more our minds are muddled by misconceptions, illusions, and falsehoods, and the less we are able to determine the correct course of action to lead our lives, to make good or wise decisions. Finding the right decision or a wise decision by which to lead our lives is to be dedicated to reality and to be truthful. Our view of reality is like a map that we have to draw, and this map has to be true and accurate. If it is, we will know who we are, where we are, what we want in life, and where we want to go, and, generally, the map will teach us how to get there: by our paying full attention to ourselves, others, and the world and by being dedicated to truth. If the map is inaccurate or false, then we are generally lost in this world.

Many of us, to a greater or lesser degree, choose to ignore reality and look for an easy route, an unrealistic path that only seems to enable us to face the problems in our lives. Most of us do not have any maps drawn, and we do not want to make any effort to draw to the paths that might help us live our lives or reach our destination. If we do have plans, most of us want our maps to be easy or plans to be simple; we do not face reality. These maps are usually quite sketchy and misleading. Some of us stop growing up in adolescence, as our maps are not well drawn and are misleading. By the end of middle age, some have given up any effort to do any more planning. In middle age, many of us no longer have any interest in new information or directions. These people are usually too tired to make any plans to face reality. Only a small percentage of us continue to grow until death by exploring reality, which is always changing and enlarging. These are the fortunate ones who are always redefining and refining their reality and their understanding of the world. They do this by having full faith in and dedication to truth and reality.

The world is constantly changing. Nothing stays the same. Cultures come and go. Technology is changing quickly. Sometimes we have too little technology, but now we have too much technology. Our position in the world is also constantly changing. When we are children, we are dependent on our parents, and, when we are adults, although we may be doubtful, it is important to face reality and be truthful in order to be powerful. When we are old, we become powerless and dependent again. This is another truth or reality that we have to face. Children and adolescents, the poor and the rich, the sick and the healthy: all see the world differently. Besides these different perspectives, each of us is bombarded with new information every day as to the nature of reality, and we have to incorporate all of this information continuously into our lives and revise our maps to reach our destination by sticking to the truth.

Sometimes, we have new information, and we have to make revisions in our plans. The process of making revisions, particularly major revisions, in our lives may be painful, but it is for our own good that we have to revise our maps.

When we have drawn a map of our lives and have a working view of the world, then we are confronted with new information, and, in view of that, the map we had drawn needs to be redrawn. This is a painful experience. Most of us become frightened and sometimes unconsciously or even consciously ignore the new information. The act of ignoring the new information is dangerous. If do ignore it, we often attempt to manipulate the world to conform to our own view of reality rather than trying to change the map. We try to destroy the new information given to us, to refuse the new reality. Such people expend much more energy defending their outdated or outmoded views of the world, views that they have acquired mostly in their childhood or adolescence, and they do not have the capacity to change or accept the reality of this world.

The process of clinging to an outmoded view of reality is the basis for many of the mental illnesses described by psychiatrists. One term they use is "transference." In psychoanalysis, transference means the process whereby emotions are passed on or displaced from one person to another. So, more generally, transference means using in adulthood the subtle ways of corresponding to the world that an individual developed during childhood, transferring to a boss or a psychiatrist, for example, the feelings one had for parents.

Transference is a big problem not only between parents and children but also between husbands and wives, between employers and employees, between friends, between different groups of people, and even between nations. We can speculate that transference issues come into play in international affairs because our leaders are human beings; they had childhoods and childhood experiences that shaped them into adults. If they had loving parents and a good childhood with a normal reality map and not feelings and experiences skewed because of transference, then they probably became good leaders. But we have examples of leaders such as Hitler, who had a bad childhood and a skewed map of reality, which led to the Second World War and the massacre of millions of innocent people.

If the truths or realities of the world are avoided, then we also feel pain. However, it is painful to face reality too. The only way we can revise our maps is by having the discipline to work on the pain. With such discipline, we should be dedicated to the truth and the ever-changing reality of this world. We must consider our personal discomfort to be relatively unimportant. We should always be searching for the truth in the ever-changing world around us.

Total dedication to truth means that, first of all, our lives are ones of continuous, never-ending self-examination. We know the world only through our relationship to it. Therefore, to know the world, we must not only examine it but also simultaneously examine ourselves all of the time. A life of total dedication to truth also means that we live our lives with the willingness to be personally challenged by others. The only way this can be done is by having ourselves open to criticism, so we have the potential to make a positive change in ourselves. The tendency to avoid challenges is so common in us that it can be considered a characteristic of human nature. Another characteristic of human nature, though, is our capacity to change and adapt, to transcend and transform ourselves according to circumstances. For people to be open to challenge and criticism, it is necessary that their maps of reality be truly open for inspection by others. A life of total dedication to truth also means, therefore, a life of total honesty. It means a continuous and never-ending process of self examination to assure that our communications with others are not only honest in the words we say but also in our actions, which should reflect, as much as is humanly possible, truth. This kind of honesty does not come painlessly because people lie to avoid the pain of challenge and its consequences.

President Nixon's lying about Watergate or President George W. Bush's lying about the weapons of mass destruction is no different than a 5-year-old child trying to hide from his parents after breaking something just to avoid legitimate suffering. People go to great lengths to avoid pain and legitimate suffering, and they will attempt to circumvent an obstacle or problem, looking for an easier path, a short cut. This will always prevent human mental and spiritual growth. It is proper that, as human beings, we should grow mentally and spiritually as much as possible, but we should not avail ourselves of any legitimate short cuts to personal mental and spiritual growth. The key word is legitimate, and we all know what legitimate suffering is in our hearts. As human beings, we have a tendency to avoid legitimate suffering. We always try to take short cuts, and these prevent our inner mental and spiritual growth.

When we try to prevent legitimate suffering, we lie, not only to others but also to ourselves. The challenges of life are our own adjustments from our own conscience, and our own realistic perception of any situation may be painful, a challenge itself, but we have to stand up and face the truth. That is the only way we can grow spiritually.

Lies are of two types—black and white. Black lies are statements we know are definitely false, even as we make them. A white lie is a statement that is not, in itself, false, at least when it is uttered, but that leaves a very significant part of the truth out of the scenario. The fact is that white lies are not any less untruthful than black lies, or any more excusable. White lies may be as destructive as black lies. Governments that hold essential or important information from the people by way of censorship of the media are no more democratic than the nations that are open but the media and press are not censored completely.

White lies in the Western world are socially acceptable. Many of us in relationships do not want to hurt another's feelings, and therefore we hide a lot of things from our loved ones. For instance, we try to hide from our children or parents our financial problems so that they do not get hurt by knowing about our financial troubles. But it is not a wise thing to hide anything from our families because, sooner or later, the truth comes out. It is better to be open about circumstances, especially ones involving finances, so family members can have good rational look themselves at the whole family situation. For some parents, the desire to protect their children is motivated by genuine but misguided love. For others, however, the loving desire to protect their children is more of a cover-up and a rationalization of

a desire to avoid being challenged by the children, and a desire to maintain authority over the children. Such parents tell their children that, being my child, you should stay a child and leave all of the adult concerns up to us. They see themselves as strong and loving parents. Of course, it is good to have the goal of being strong and loving parents in front of us, but, unless we look deeper into what this image actually entails and refrain from pretending to protect our children, on the one hand, while lying to them and keeping them in a state of ignorance, on the other, we are misguided."
What rules should be followed? What to do if one is dedicated to truth? First, never speak falsehoods. Two, bear in mind that actively withholding the truth is always potentially a lie and that, in each instance in which the truth is withheld, a significant moral decision is definitely required. Three, the decision to withhold the truth should never be based on personal need such as the need for power. Four, the decision to withhold the truth must always be based entirely upon the needs of the person or people from whom the truth is being withheld. Five, the assessment of the other person's needs is an act of responsibility that is so complex that it can only be executed wisely when one operates with genuine love for the other person. Six, the primary factor in the assessment of the other person's needs is if the assessment of that person's capacity is to utilize the truth for his or her own spiritual and mental growth. In assessing the capacity of another person to utilize the truth for personal spiritual growth, it should be borne in mind that it is best to underestimate rather than overestimate the capacity of the other person.

Making the correct assessment can often be a burden, but it is the never-ending burden of self-discipline that is very important, which is why most people offer a life with limited honesty and openness and a relatively closed nature rather than an openness that maps their lives to the world. It is easier to hide than to open our life maps to others. Yet the rewards of honesty and dedication to truth are great, though demanding: great by virtue of the fact that honest maps of our lives are open to people who want to grow mentally and spiritually but demanding because these maps are continuously being challenged. Through this openness, we can establish and maintain close and intimate relationships with people far more efficiently than those who are not as open, who are considered to be closed people. People who are open-minded are totally free, and they are not burdened by any need to hide. They do not have any shadows following them. They do not have to construct a new life to hide an old life, as we see with people who hide things and who have closed attitudes. People with open attitudes are the ones who do not waste any effort in hiding things. They are true and open and are guided by the dignity of truth. They do not have to waste time or effort in covering their tracks to maintain disguises, as we see in people who hide things and have closed attitudes. People with open-mindedness who are dedicated to truth ultimately have the energy for the self-discipline of honesty, which takes far less energy than does the secretiveness we see in people with closed attitudes when they hide things from their loved ones. The more honest one gets, the easier it is to continue to be honest in life. It is also far easier to live a very happy and balanced life. The more lies one has to tell, the more it is necessary for that person to lie again. Therefore, these people who lie continue to lie, and they have to manipulate their whole world. The people who are dedicated to truth are the people with openness, and their dedication to truth lives a life in the open. These people who are dedicated to truth show courage; they live as open human beings, and they become free from fear because they do not have to hide anything from anyone, as they are totally dedicated to truth, mentally and spiritually.

4. *Living a Balanced Life*

Balancing is a discipline that gives flexibility to our life. Balancing is required for successful living in every year of life. For example, anger is an emotion that has evolved in order to allow humans to survive. It is seen in the animal kingdom for survival. Without anger, it is well known that the animals would be stepped on until exterminated. Only with anger can the animal kingdom survive. More often than not, we perceive others as attempting to encroach on our territory, but then we realize, on close examination, that they are not encroaching and their intentions are not of encroachment. But we perceive their actions as encroaching upon our territories. When we determine that people are truly intending to encroach on our territory, then, in our best interest, we respond with anger. To function in this complex world, it is necessary for us to have the capacity not only to express our anger but also to hold it and not to express it. We must possess the capacity to express our anger in different ways, as well as to control it when it is not necessary.

At times, it is necessary to express our anger only after much deliberation. At other times, it is more to our benefit to express it immediately and spontaneously, if we feel that we are being encroached upon unnecessarily. Sometimes, it is best to express it in a calm way, and, other times, it is all right to express anger loudly and hotly. Therefore, not only do we need to know how to deal with our anger in different ways, at different times, and in different situations and scenarios, but also we need to understand how to match the right time with the right style of expression of our anger.

To handle our anger with competence, we should have flexibility of mind, and we should have a flexible response system in which to show our anger appropriately when it is appropriate. Therefore, it is no wonder that handling anger is a complex task. It is usually accomplished by adulthood, or even mid life. Some people, however, will go through the whole of life without being able to control their anger.

People who suffer from an inadequately flexible mind are the ones who are unable to control their anger. These are the people who are generally crippled with guilt, anxiety, and insecurity. It is very difficult for them to have a flexible mind to respond to different scenarios or situations, especially when anger is the natural response.

Therefore, mental health requires an extraordinary capacity for a flexible mind, and it is a delicate balance between, say, a conflicting need and the responsibilities, duties, and directions one has to take at different stages in life. The sense of self-discipline is called balancing. Balancing is also a way of giving up a few things in life and accepting the new evolved nature of our being. Balancing is a discipline, and it is the act of giving something up that is usually painful. We are usually unwilling to suffer the pain of giving up our excessive needs and, at times, certain behaviour. We usually learn in our life that the loss of balance will ultimately be more painful than giving up what we must let go in order to maintain balance. In one way or another, it is a lesson we learn continuously throughout life. As we negotiate the curves and corners of our lives, we have to continuously give up part of ourselves, some of our excessive needs and some of our behaviours, exchanging these for more realistic needs and actions by way of balancing. We have alternative routes, different things to give up and different ways of balancing while travelling on the journey of life.

So far, we have talked about giving up our childish nature and attitudes, and our excessive needs and behaviours, to have a balanced life, a process that is usually painful but very important as we travel on our journey of life. We have to give up childhood attitudes, and doing so leads to mental and spiritual maturity. Now let us turn to the well-established patterns of behaviour, to ideologies and personality traits, which one must give up when one matures spiritually and mentally. The feelings associated with giving up something that we dearly loved are painful, and sometimes, these feelings can lead us into depression. Because, as human beings, we continuously grow (and we have to grow to have mental maturity), depression, at times, is a natural process, itself a part of growing up mentally and spiritually. We have to get rid of our old self, which is an integral part of the process of growing mentally and spiritually. Depression is normal in this scenario. As normal, healthy human beings, we have to become abnormal and deal with depression at times, which is a part of the giving up process. The length of the depression is usually not prolonged if we continually grow mentally. The completion of this process leads to being a better person.

There are many factors that interfere with the process of growing up, and these, too, can lead to depression and, sometimes, to a prolonged chronic pathological depression. One of the most common factors that leads to chronic pathological depression is the pattern of experiences in childhood, a pattern in which either the parents or fate are responsible for the chronic pathological depression. The needs of the child are not met in the proper way with love and attention. That creates a tendency for clinging to pleasure patterns and avoiding the pain or loss of the giving up process. For this reason, pathologic depression involves blockages in the giving up process. I believe that this type of chronic depression has its central root of traumatic injury in a childhood where basic needs are not met, so the capacity to give up gradually is not acquired due to the lack of love or because of bad parenting or even bad fate.

We hear this term, mid-life crisis, quite frequently. It is basically the problem of not giving up, of not having a normal development of mental and spiritual growth, and of not having a balanced way of life. As Erik Erikson taught us about 50 years ago, we go through a transition period in our life cycle that is problematic and painful in that we have to successfully work our way through giving up cherished notions and old ways of doing things; we have to change ourselves willingly. This giving up process is important if we are to grow up. Yet we constantly cling to old patterns of thinking and old behaviours, failing to negotiate with any new crises, which truly requires growing up, and to experience the joyful sense of rebirth that accompanies a successful transformation of our old self into a new, mature, greater self.

The desires and attitudes that should be given up during the course of life if we are to evolve wholly and successfully are

1. yearning for the state of infancy in which no external demands are made on us
2. the fantasy of omnipotence
3. the desire for total possession of one's parents
4. the dependency of childhood
5. distorted images of one's parents
6. the omnipotentiality of adolescence
7. the freedom of non-commitment

8. the agility of youth
9. the sexuality, attractiveness, or potency of youth
10. the fantasy of immortality
11. authority over one's children
12. various forms of temporal power
13. the independence of physical health
14. ultimately, the self in life, itself

These are the growing up or giving up processes at every stage in life. We have to grow by giving up our old attitudes in order to mature and to be a better human being. The process of giving up requires the phenomenon of love. For most of us, it is a gradual process. It is a kind of discipline that is also called "bracketing." Bracketing is essentially an act of balancing the need for stability and for the assertion of our self with the knowledge and understanding that, by temporally giving up one's self, so to speak, one makes room for a better self. This discipline is very well described by a theologian, Sam Keen, in his book *To a Dancing God*.

> The second step requires that I go beyond the idiosyncratic and egocentric perception of immediate experience. Mature awareness is possible only when I have digested and compensated for the biases and prejudices that are the residue of my personal history. Awareness of what presents itself to me involves a double movement of attention, silencing the familiar and welcoming the strange. Each time I approach a strange object, person or event, I have a tendency to let my present needs, past experiences or expectations for the future determine what I will see. If I am to appreciate the uniqueness of any datum, I must be sufficiently aware of my frequency of ideas and characteristic emotional distortions to bracket them long enough to welcome the strangeness and novelty into my perceptual world. This discipline of bracketing, compensating or silencing requires sophisticated self-knowledge and courageous honesty. Yet, without this discipline, each present moment is only the repetition of something already seen or experienced. In order for genuine novelty to emerge, for the unique presence of things, persons or events to take root in me, I must undergo a decentralization of ego.
> *Sam Keen*[7]

Bracketing is a disciple that illustrates the consequences of giving up and growing up, namely giving up our old selves and growing into our new selves, which is a discipline of self. It is a self-enlarging process. The pain of giving up is actually the pain of growing old. There is pain in growing old, as we realize that it is inevitable. Birth and death are on different sides of the same coin. It is not unreasonable to pay closer attention to this process of life when one contemplates death. In the West, the concept of reincarnation is not real, but, when we are willing to entertain the possibility of some kind of rebirth, agreeing, simultaneously, that "in the midst of life we are in death," it is clear that this lifetime is actually a series of concurrent deaths and births. In life, one must continue to learn to live, as Seneca said very well two centuries ago: "From all things learn to live and die."[9] It is also clear that the further one travels on the journey of life, the more one experiences birth and death, and also joy and pain.

When the suffering is completely accepted, it ceases to be suffering, as you have accepted it with your disciplined mind. Finally, the answer to a spiritually evolved person will be a life of extraordinary love. With this extraordinary love comes an extraordinary joy of life. The best measure of a person's greatness is the capacity of that person to accept suffering as a way of life and to evolve into a better person. Buddha and Christ are the names of people who suffered in life to understand the joy of life. They have left us such great messages in their teachings from which we can learn and grow and accept suffering as a way of life, a path towards becoming a good human being.

If your goal is to avoid pain and suffering, then I would advise you not to seek a higher level of consciousness or spiritual growth. One cannot achieve a higher level of consciousness or spiritual growth without suffering. Suffering, though painful, is demanded of us. When you have grown and evolved, then, and only then, does suffering itself become easy to handle. The simple pleasures of life become extremely joyful.

1.Benjamin Franklin, quoted in M. Scott Peck, *The Road Less Traveled*, 25th ed. (New York: Simon and Schuster Inc., 2003), 16.

2. Carl Jung, *Psychology and Religion: West and East*, trans. R. F. C. Hull, vol. 2 of the *Collected Works*, Bollinger Series No. 20, 2nd ed. (Princeton, NJ: Princeton University Press, 1973), 75.

3. Although this adage is often expressed in exactly these words and is attributed to political activist Eldridge Cleaver, what he really said in a 1968 speech is "What we're saying today is that you're either part of the solution or you're part of the problem." Speech to San Francisco Barristers' Club, San Francisco, CA, September 1968.

4. Gregory J. P. Godek, *Confessions of a True Romantic* (Naperville, IL: Sourcebooks Casablanca, 2003), 179

5. Robert Browning, "Fra Lippo Lippi," *Selections from Poetical Works* (London: Smith, Elder & Co., 1874), 197.

6. Anthony Robbins, *Awaken the Giant Within* (New York: Simon & Schuster, 1992), 508

7. Sam Keen, *To The Dancing God* (New York: Harper and Row, 1970), 28.

8. *The Annotated Book of Common Prayer*, ed. John Henry Blunt (London: Rivingtons, 1872), 297.

9. *Miscellanies Moral and Instructive, in Prose and Verse*, ed. Milcah Martha Moore (London: J. Phillips, 1787), 25.

CHAPTER 4

Contentment

People are always searching for happiness in treasures,
but truly it is hidden in contentment.
Prophet Mohammed

When Prophet Mohammed was 40 years of age, he founded Islam in 610 AD. This great message, which is written in his teachings (the Hadith), tells us that people are always searching for happiness in money, wealth, and treasures but that, truly, happiness is hidden in contentment. This great human being, who was most humble, lived 1,400 years ago, and he shows us that we should open our minds and hearts and look for happiness in contentment rather than searching for it endlessly, fruitlessly in money and treasures.

Our feeling of contentment is strongly influenced by our tendency to compare. We are constantly comparing ourselves in our current situations with ourselves of the past or comparing ourselves to our colleagues or friends. Constant comparison with those who are smarter or more beautiful or more successful than we are also tends to breed envy, frustration, and unhappiness. But we can use this simple principle in a positive way. We can increase our feeling of satisfaction by comparing ourselves to those who are less fortunate and also by reflecting on all the other things we have compared to others who have less.

In today's world, we are always wanting more and more. We want better, then the best, and the better than most. This quest for more and better has become our focus.

A question was asked to Prophet Mohammed, and it is mentioned in the Hadith. "Who is the richest man in the world?" He answered, "Be contented, and you will be the richest man in the world." This teaching, passed down to us from 1,400 years ago, came from one of the greatest men who ever lived. He gives us this message from those times, a message so very real in our present time in this world. Things are changing so fast, and everyone is competing and wants to be the best. They want to show their wealth and riches by getting more and more things; they put pressure on themselves in every way—every minute and every second—just trying to become more of themselves. But, honestly, the richest man in the world is the one who is content and happy with what he has and with whom he has become.

Prophet Mohammed was also asked who is the most just man in the world. He answered, "Desire for others what you desire for yourself, and you will be the most just of men." This describes that if you desire something good and great for yourself, then you should also desire the same for others.

He was asked who the best of men in this world are. His response: "Do good to others, and you will be the best of men." This sage and saint was a most humble man, telling us 1,400 years ago all of these teachings that are so very important in this day and age—to be humble and kind, to be thankful for what we have, and to be content with what we have become.

We can increase or decrease our sense of life satisfaction by changing our perspective, which clearly points to the supremacy of one's mental outlook in living a happy life.

There is a reference in Buddhist literature to four factors of happiness or fulfillment.

- Health
- Worldly satisfaction
- Spirituality
- Enlightenment

Together, they embrace the totality of an individual's quest for happiness.

> Give me beauty in the inward soul; and may the outward and inward man be as one.
>
> *Socrates*[1]

Good health is considered to be one of the necessary or important factors for a happy life. Another source of happiness is material facilities or wealth. One other factor is having friendships or companions in order to enjoy a fulfilled life. We keep a good circle of friends with whom we can relate emotionally and whom we can trust.

The most important thing to being happy and to enjoying a happy, fulfilled life is your state of mind, which is the key—and that is very crucial.

Just underneath that beautiful surface of affluence is a kind of mental unrest leading to frustration, unnecessary quarrels, or reliance on drugs and alcohol. In the worse cases, this turbulence leads even to suicide. There are no guarantees that wealth alone can give you the joy of fulfillment in life that you are seeking. If you have hateful thoughts and anger, somewhere deep down within your self, then these will ruin your health. They also destroy happiness. If you are mentally unhappy or frustrated, then physical comfort is not much help. On the other hand, if you can maintain a calm, peaceful state of mind, then you can be a very happy person—even if you have poor health or are without possessions. And having things does not guarantee serenity or security. In an intense moment of anger or hatred, you feel like throwing or breaking all the wonderful possessions you have gained. In that moment, your possessions mean nothing. Today, societies are very developed materially, yet many people are not very happy.

If we utilize our health and wealth in a positive way by helping others, this use will be a contributory factor in achieving a happier life. Still, without the right mental attitude, health, wealth, or using both to help others has very little impact on our long-term feelings of happiness. Peace of mind is very important, and we have to take this factor very seriously in our daily life. The greater the level of calmness of our mind, the greater is our peace of mind, and the greater is our ability to enjoy a happier and fulfilled, joyful life.

A calm state of mind or peace of mind should not be confused with an insensitive or apathetic state of mind. Having a calm or peaceful state of mind does not mean that we are totally spaced out or empty; this serene state of mind is rooted in affection and compassion. The peaceful person has a high level of sensitivity and inner good feeling; he or she wants to help others with affection and compassion. If you possess the inner quality of a calm mind and a degree of stability within it, even if you lack various external facilities or materialistic things, you can still live a happy and joyful life.

> Charity and personal force are the only investments worth any thing.
> *Walt Whitman*[2]

Western cultures are based on material acquisitions. Success is also measured by material accumulation and display. We are surrounded and constantly bombarded with advertisements promoting the latest things such as cars and televisions and so on. We all have desires. There are two kinds of desires: positive and negative. Positive desires are for those things that bring true happiness, such as peace, harmony, friendliness, and caring.

The other kind of desire is negative, and, sometimes, it can be unreasonable, such as when we constantly buy new things we don't need. We are surrounded and influenced by other people that have all of these materialistic things. For instance, every year hundreds of new vehicles are available, and we see our friend or colleague driving a new model car, and we want to have one too, but it is not really feasible to change your car every year if you can't afford it, and it is also not necessary to do so. In the Western world, a car is a necessity. In a village in India or Africa, there are no cars at all, and, if you take a car there, then it becomes a burden on you rather than a necessary aid, as you can more easily travel on bicycles or even by walking short distances.

Self-satisfaction alone cannot determine if the desire is positive or negative. Mental attitudes that just want more and more eventually reach a limit. When people reach this limit, there is actually a negative consequence, and they go into a depression. This is a very real danger inherent in this type of desire for self-satisfaction to the extent of overindulgence, so people find unhappiness rather than contentment by buying or acquiring new and modern things as they come onto the market.

> The secret of success is learning how to use pain and pleasure instead of having pain and pleasure using you. If you do that, you are in control of your life. If you don't, life controls you.
> *Anthony Robbins*[3]

Excessive desire leads to greed. This is an exaggerated form of desire. When desire becomes so intense that even after fulfilling this desire, one is still not content, aspiration becomes the greed to acquire more and more. When a person gets into this kind of attitude, then longing becomes limitless and bottomless and leads to more trouble. One interesting thing about greed is that the underlying motive is to seek satisfaction, but, ironically, even after obtaining the object of desire, the person motivated by greed is still not satisfied. The true antidote to greed is contentment. If you have a strong sense of contentment, it doesn't matter whether you obtain the object or not. Either way, you are still content.

> Wealth is the product of man's capacity to think.
> *Ayn Rand*[4]

Inner contentment is very important. There are two methods to achieve inner contentment. One method is to acquire everything one really wants, such as money, houses, cars, a perfect partner, and a perfect, healthy body. But this method, if it goes unchecked, will result in an endless, unattainable goal. The second and more reliable method of achieving contentment is to appreciate what we have.

Most of us are aware of the story of Christopher Reeve—the actor who was thrown from his horse in 1995 and suffered a spinal cord injury, which left him completely paralyzed from the neck down with quadriplegia. He was on mechanical ventilation for a long time, although, because of his willpower, he was able to breath without a respirator for thirty minutes about seven months after his accident. His initial response to his injury was utmost despair, but, relatively quickly, this passed because of his strong mind. He found he could cope with such a disastrous accident. He cited that he had the blessings of his lovely wife and children, who were very supportive, which enabled him to cope.

He realized that the only way he could go through the rest of his life was to look at his assets: that is, his strong mind and very positive attitude towards life. Because of these assets, he made very good progress over the years until he died in early October of 2004. Christopher Reeve elected to use his mind to increase awareness and educate the public about spinal cord injuries for the almost ten years during which he lived after his accident, and he also spoke and wrote about his life and continued to direct and work in films and television.

> Things do not change; we change.
> *Henry David Thoreau*[5]

We have seen how our mental outlook is more effective as a means of achieving happiness rather than seeking it through external sources such as wealth, position, and even physical health. The internal sources of happiness are closely linked with an inner feeling of contentment. It is a sense of self worth.

> For it is not enough to have a good mind; the main thing is to apply it well.
> *René Descartes*[6]

A perfect example of the excellent application of a good spiritual mind is the Dalai Lama, who is the Tibetan priest who was thrown out of his country by the Chinese. He has been living in India for a number of years. He lost his country, his political authority in Tibet, and he even became a refugee. While he was in Tibet, he had some political authority. But now he is a refugee in India, and he has no political authority there. Still you will find that this man has inner contentment and a sense of self worth, which keep him happy. He describes in his books that the big bond he has is that he is a human being living within the human community, which gives him a sense of fulfilment and happiness.

> Experience is not what happens to a man; it is what a man does with what happens to him.
> *Aldous Huxley*[7]

The human bond is enough to give rise to a sense of worth and dignity. This bond can become a source of consolation, even in the event that you lose everything else. The Dalai Lama quoted in his books that two types of individuals exist. One is wealthy and successful, surrounded by relatives and friends. However, if that person's source of dignity and self worth is only material, then this individual can sustain a sense of security only so long as he or she has fortune. But the moment that fortune leaves, the person will suffer because there is no other refuge. The other type of person enjoys similar economic status and financial success, but at the same time, is warm and affectionate with a feeling of compassion. This person has another sense of worth, one outside of material security—another source that gives him or her a sense of dignity, another anchor, so there is less chance of that person becoming depressed even upon the loss of fortune. Through this type of reasoning, you can see the very practical value of human warmth and affection in developing an inner worth.

> Every great and commanding moment in the annals of the world is the triumph of some enthusiasm.
> *Ralph Waldo Emerson*[8]

What is the difference between happiness and pleasure? Pleasure is something that is not long lasting and is unstable. For example, sexual activity can give us pleasure, but the pleasure does not last long. It does not give us inner happiness, which is long lasting. Happiness can be achieved through contentment and feeling inner worth. Most of us confuse happiness and pleasure, and we think that continuous pleasure can make a person happy. This is not true. One may not be able to enjoy sex or other pleasures as one grows older, but true happiness relates more to the mind and heart. It is a general and lasting happiness that keeps a person happy deep inside. This is true contentment and inner worth.

We are faced every day with numerous decisions and choices. Often the right choice is a difficult one or the one that involves some sacrifice of our pleasure. Many philosophers, theologians, and psychologists have explored our relationship with pleasure. In the third century BC, Epicurus based his system of ethics on the bold assertion that pleasure is the beginning and end of the blessed life. But Epicurus did not advocate an "Eat, drink, and be merry, for tomorrow we die" philosophy. Actually, this saying is based on biblical verses from Ecclesiastes, Isaiah, and Luke. Epicurus understood pleasure or happiness as a tranquillity of soul, which comes from the moderate and prudent pursuit of virtue and philosophy, and he acknowledges that unbridled devotion to pleasure could sometimes lead to pain instead.

> And, according to Epicurus, I conceive that pleasures are to be avoided if greater pains be the consequence; and pains to be coveted that will terminate in greater pleasures.
> *Michel de Montaigne*[9]

In the nineteenth century, Sigmund Freud formulated his own theory about pleasure. According to Freud, a sentimental motivating force for the entire psychic apparatus was the wish to relieve tension caused by unfulfilled sexual drive. In other words, our underlying motive is to seek pleasure.

We all know and feel the wonder of that special touch or smile from a loved one and the luxury of a hot bath on a cold, rainy day, and many of us have also experienced an alcohol buzz, the bliss of unrestrained sexual activity, or the exhilaration of winning the lottery or at a casino. These are all very real pleasures, but they are temporary. Fortunately, we have a place to begin—the simple reminder that we are seeking a life with inner happiness. As we approach our choices in life, keeping this search in mind, it is easier to give up things that are ultimately harmful to us, even if these things bring us momentary pleasure.

> Seeing is believing, but feeling is the truth.
> *Thomas Fuller*[10]

We should be seeking ultimate happiness, a kind of happiness that is stable and persistent. This is a state of happiness that remains despite life's ups and downs and the normal fluctuation of moods; this happiness is a part of the very matrix of our being. With this perspective, it is easier to make the right decisions because we are choosing inner happiness and not denying or withholding it from ourselves—we have an attitude of moving towards rather than moving away, an attitude of embracing life rather than rejecting it. This underlying sense of moving towards happiness can have a very profound effect. It makes us more receptive and more open to the joy of living.

Nature has placed mankind under the governance of two sovereign masters, pain and pleasure.... They govern us in all we do, in all we say, in all we think: every effort we can make to throw off our subjection will serve but to demonstrate and confirm it.
Jeremy Bentham[11]

Spirituality and Enlightenment

Before enlightenment—chopping wood, carrying water. After enlightenment—chopping wood, carrying water.
Zen proverb

Zen Buddhism was founded in China in the sixth century and became widespread in Japan by the twelfth century. It emphasizes achieving enlightenment by the most direct possible means.

The message of this famous proverb is that enlightenment is not an attainment but rather a realization. Once you have reached this realization, everything appears to have changed, yet you see no change has taken place in the world or in your surroundings. You live the same life you had been living before enlightenment; that is you do your regular work—whatever you had been doing. It is only that you had been going through life with your eyes closed, and now they are open. Now you can see; the world hasn't changed but you simply view it differentially—in a new light. This proverb about chopping wood and carrying water says to us that enlightenment does not begin on any high mountain but takes place exactly where you are, whatever you are doing, and it is only that you have realized this change in you. You feel life, and you experience the world with new vision. There is a sense of well-being and peace associated with this changed circumstance. It is what you are experiencing with enlightenment.

If I am stressed, anxious, fearful, or tense, then I am not realizing the potential that I can be enlightened or receive enlightenment in that moment. An enlightened person, I believe, has learned to be aware of the non-peaceful moment. He or she is the wise one who realizes his or her ignorance while others, who are unaware of their ignorance, are truly ignorant.

The fool doth think he is wise; but the wise man knows himself to be a fool.
Shakespeare [11]

In recent years, I have developed a sense of inner peace, but still I have to "chop wood and carry water"—to sustain myself as I have done for all of the years during which I have been practicing medicine. Every day, I still have to get up in the morning, go the hospital and do rounds, see sick people, then go to the office and see patients all day in consultation. Each day I have to exercise, stay healthy, eat proper meals, brush my teeth, and so on. I must look after my family and pay the bills. I have the same basic concerns—how to protect my family, feed them, advise them, and deal with them. I still have to chop wood and carry water as a member of the family. Enlightenment is not a means of eliminating daily chores but rather a change in your outlook on life. We have to live the same life as before. Enlightenment only changes how you see the things around you; it gives you a new perspective.

Enlightenment will not change your outer world, but it will let you see the world in a new light. You only know one way of processing the same old world. For instance, parenting. Previously I believed that my children could rule my emotional life. But now I see my children and their attitudes in a new fashion. I am compelled to join with them in their emotional conduct. I see the success that all of my children are experiencing. I have a more detached perspective. Detachment is not an attitude of indifference; rather, it is knowing I have the power to choose peace for myself in every moment. I still have some activities, problems, and even chores each day. As long as I am physically fit, I will continue to chop wood and carry water. Nothing has changed in this regard. However, a new way of approaching problems is what constitutes spirituality and enlightenment.

Spirituality and enlightenment are not things that will set you free, but rather they will connect you more profoundly to all you see. You begin to treat all the tasks, even the most difficult task, as opportunities to know God. You see things in a different light. You bring peace to everything you see. You become more aware of things around you. You become less preoccupied labelling things. Different names of flowers and trees become less important than actually experiencing them.

The simple Zen proverb of chopping wood and carrying water has been handed down for hundreds of years to the seekers of spirituality and enlightenment. It is a great gift to us. We should learn from it and follow this simple philosophy—lead the same life and live in the same world, but see the world with new vision and new light. This is what constitutes enlightenment.

We should let go of our inclination to see enlightenment as something we achieve at a future time in our lives, when circumstances are better. The future time is no time. The right time is the present time—the present moment. We should have this inclination of becoming more enlightened and seeing life from a new perspective now. It is important that we reserve time and space within ourselves for enlightenment—especially in moments when we are typically anxious or worried.

Finally, we should become aware of our own ignorance as it is revealed each day to us. Do not ignore ignorance or blame it on circumstances but recognize that enlightened ones are those who know that they are ignorant. The ignorant ones are unaware of their ignorance, so become aware of your ignorance.

---

1. Socrates quoted in Plato, "Phaedrus," in *The Dialogues of Plato*, ed. Benjamin Jowett (Oxford: Clarendon Press, 1875), 159.
2. Walt Whitman, Leaves of Grass (Philadelphia: D. McKay, 1884), 290.
3. Anthony Robbins, *Awaken the Giant Within* (New York: Simon & Schuster, 1992), 54.
4. Ayn Rand, *Atlas Shrugged* (New York: New American Library, 1957), 371.
5. Henry David Thoreau, *Walden* (New Haven, CT: Yale University Press, 2004), 319.
6. René Descartes, *Discourse on Method* (Indianapolis, IN: Hackett Publishing, 1998), 1.
7. Aldous Huxley, *Texts and Pretexts* (London, Chatto & Windus, 1933), 5.
8. Ralph Waldo Emerson, "Man the Reformer: A lecture read before the Mechanics' Apprentices' Library Association, Boston, January 25, 1841," *Essays and Lectures* (New York, Library of America, 1983), 147.
9. Michel de Montaigne, *Essays of Michel Seigneur de Montaigne* (London: Daniel Brown, J. Nicholson, R. Wellington, B. Tooke, B. Barker, 1711), 646.
10. Thomas Fuller, quoted in Tian Dayton, *Daily Affirmations for Parents* (Deerfield Beach, FL: Health Communications, 1991), 20.
11. Jeremy Bentham, *An Introduction to the Principles of Morals and Legislation*, ed. J. H. Burns and H. L. A. Hart (1970; repr., London: Routledge, 1982), 11.
12. Shakespeare, *As You Like It*, 5.1.30–31.

CHAPTER 5

Mind or Consciousness

Imagination is more important than knowledge.
Albert Einstein[1]

Identifying one's mental status is a very important factor in achieving happiness. Our basic needs, such as food, clothing, and shelter, must obviously be met first, and, after that, it is very important to know one's state of mind to achieve complete happiness. One day my daughter Noreen brought me a painting, which showed a nice picture of a golf course with these words written underneath: "It matters how long you drive your golf ball, but it is more important that you know yourself and enjoy life." In those days, I was working very hard, and she probably saw me stressed at times and felt that I should slow down and smell the roses—look around, play golf, and be happy and enjoy life. It is very important to know one's self. Most of us have needs. Some of us have basic needs, and we are happy with whatever we have, but some others are not happy even if they have everything. They try to fulfil their needs by achieving or by accumulating wealth or material things, thinking that doing these things will make them happy. Unfortunately, achieving material gain will not achieve complete happiness.

> Give me but one firm spot on which to stand, and I will move the earth.
> Archimedes on the action of a lever[2]

When we talk about mind or consciousness, then, we consider thousands of different thoughts. Some of these thoughts are very useful and positive, but some are negative or very harmful. These negative thoughts are the thoughts in need of review. The first step in seeking happiness is learning to identify the positive thoughts and the negative thoughts. We first have to learn how negative emotions are harmful to us, and how positive emotions are helpful. We should also realize that negative emotions are harmful not only to one's personality but also to society and to the future of this world. This realization enhances our determination to face and overcome them. Then, there is the realization of the beneficial aspects of positive emotions and behaviours. Once we realize these benefits, we become determined to cherish, develop, and increase positive emotions, no matter how difficult it may be. A kind of spontaneous willingness from within will help us to achieve happiness through this process. The process of analyzing our thoughts and emotions is beneficial, as it is very important to differentiate between the positive and the negative emotions—those that are harmful to us and those that are beneficial to us. The secret of my happiness is my own good fortune, as well as the power of positive thinking.

> It is the mind that maketh good or ill,
> That maketh wretch or happy, rich or poor.
> *Edmund Spenser*[3]

My happiness is all within my head, and although I can help myself to contentment by having positive emotions to keep me happy, I have found it best to keep others happy around me. I get positive input from them as well to keep my own sanity and to maintain a very healthy and happy state of mind.

> "These virtues are formed in man by his doing the actions"; we are what we repeatedly do. Excellence, then, is not an act but a habit: "the good of man is a working of the soul in the way of excellence in a complete life ... for as it is not one swallow or one fine day that makes a spring, so it is not one day or a short time that makes a man blessed and happy."
> *Aristotle*[4]

The causal relationship between doing and being is very important. If you desire happiness, you should seek the causes that give rise to it, and if you do not want any suffering, then you should ensure that the causes and conditions that give rise to it no longer occur. So an appreciation of a causal relationship is very important in seeking happiness.

Now we will talk about the mental factor, which is very important in achieving happiness. We have to examine the variety of mental states that we experience in daily life. We need to clearly identify these different mental states and make a distinction—classifying them according to whether they lead to happiness or to suffering.

Hatred, jealousy, and anger are harmful, negative states of mind, as they destroy our well-being and mental happiness. Once you have these feelings towards others, you are filled with negative emotions Therefore, hatred and ill feelings are very harmful to us. In these kinds of emotional states, people appear hostile, and this leads to fear, inhibition, hesitation, and a sense of insecurity within others. On the contrary, mental states such as kindness and compassion are definitely very positive and very useful, and these states of mind are very important in achieving happiness.

If we have compassionate, warm, kind-hearted personalities, we express love and kindness towards others, and this automatically opens an inner door through which we can communicate very easily with other people. This resulting communication leads to a feeling of warmth, as we consider all human beings are just like us, and we can relate to them more easily. This warmth will create a spirit of friendship, so feelings of fear, self-doubt, and insecurity will automatically be dispelled when we have are compassionate, warm, and kind-hearted. Therefore, cultivating positive mental states, such as kindness and compassion, definitely leads to better psychological health.

> Hold yourself responsible for a higher standard than what anybody else expects of you.
> *Henry Ward Beecher*[5]

My Mind to Me A Kingdom Is
Sir Edward Dyer (1543–1607)

My mind to me a kingdom is,
Such present joys therein I find,
That it excels all other bliss
That world affords or grows by kind:
Though much I want which most would have,
Yet still my mind forbids to crave.

No princely pomp, no wealthy store,
No force to win the victory,
No wily wit to salve a sore,
No shape to feed a loving eye;

To none of these I yield as thrall:
For why? My mind doth serve for all.

I see how plenty surfeits oft,
And hasty climbers soon do fall;
I see that those which are aloft
Mishap doth threaten most of all;
They get with toil, they keep with fear;
Such care my mind could never bear.

Content to live, this is my stay;
I seek no more than may suffice;
I press to bear no haughty sway;
Look, what I lack my mind supplies:
Lo! thus I triumph like a king,
Content with that my mind doth bring.

Some have too much, yet still do crave;
I little have, and seek no more.
They are but poor, though much they have
And I am rich with little store;
They poor, I rich; they beg, I give;
They lack, I leave; they pine, I live.

I laugh not at another's loss;
I grudge not at another's gain;
No worldly waves my mind can toss;
My state at one doth still remain.
I fear no foe, I fawn no friend;
I loathe not life, nor dread my end.

Some weigh their pleasure by their lust,
Their wisdom by their rage of will;
Their treasure is their only trust,
A cloaked craft their store of skill:
But all the pleasure that I find
Is to maintain a quiet mind.

My wealth is health and perfect ease:
My conscience clear my chief defence;
I neither seek by bribes to please,
Nor by deceit to breed offence:
Thus do I live; thus will I die;
Would all did so as well as I![6]

Sir Edward Dyer, a sixteenth century poet who was extremely popular for his poems, is best known for his lyric beginning "My mind to me a kingdom is." Today, this poem is the only one that remains well known. I was quite impressed by this poem, and I think it is important that we learn from this great man, who was telling us about half a millennium ago about how important the potency of mind is in guiding us to live a happy life. It is important that we detach ourselves from things such as our bodies, and being in the kingdom of a quiet mind is very awesome. We feel there are no boundaries, no time or space, yet the quiet mind is always with us and guiding and directing us in every way, in virtually everything we do in our lives. This is our kingdom and we are the only ones who can use it in all circumstances to create a feeling of delight for ourselves. The mind represents our freedom—the place that cannot be invaded by others. It is a place of sanity when all around us are in turmoil. This is a wonderful, invisible mind I am talking about. We should recognize its potential with awe and appreciate it for its magnitude and vast power of thinking and imagination.

If you crave for something badly, just remind yourself of this stanza: "Yet still my mind forbids to crave." Dyer is referring to the ability of our joys. Understand that we have this power of choice; that is, nothing outside ourselves can be blamed for our cravings or our unhealthy attitudes and addictions. We should go back further—to our inner kingdom—to our mind, which is capable of making these choices that are so powerful; the mind can inhibit bad cravings or unhealthy attitudes. We should stop blaming society or people for the circumstances we find ourselves in. We should go back to the powerful kingdom of our mind, which serves the highest good for all of our concerns rather than for our self-imposed ego alone.

The habit of acquiring more and more is not necessary. To chase after success at all costs, to consistently pursue approval from others is not necessary. These cravings are all self imposed, and controlling them is the function of the invisible kingdom of the mind, as Sir Edward Dyer told us centuries ago. We should go back to our kingdom of mind and remind ourselves of what is right and what is wrong for us.

"They are but poor, though much they have / And I am rich with little store," said Sir Edward Dyer. He says that living in agony, never seeming to be satisfied, always being in pursuit of an elusive "more" is not necessary. "They lack, I leave; they pine, I live" indicates that people who are wanting more and more are not happier than others who use mind power, who are happy and content.

Sir Edward Dyer gently suggests to us that there is a choice—either to become consumed with greed and acquisition or to live with contentment and happiness, as a consequence of mind power.

As for living to get more and more and to worry about losing all, "Such care my mind could never bear." Know that it is your mind that makes these choices. Nothing more. Unlimited happiness and fulfilment are available to us, as indicated by this poem.

"Content to live, this is my stay; / I seek no more than may suffice": being inwardly content, says Sir Edward Dyer, is the key to happiness. Again, this passage is a clear indication that we have to be content with what we have, which is enough, even more than enough, and I seek no more than what my needs are. Doing this can be achieved by our mind power.

Our mind is capable of giving us a lifetime of peace and tranquillity, if we decide to change our minds and start living now. We should always be referring to this inner kingdom of the mind, to create a life of giving rather than lacking. It is our mind that is always having this freedom—this space and this peace. It is all within the mind. We go back to whenever we are faced with difficult questions or choices in our lives. Every fear we experience does not come from outside but rather from inside. It is our choice, with mind power, to sweep away fear of the unknown. We should have life-long conditioning to eliminate this fear and enable the state of grace described by Sir Edward Dyer: "I loathe not life, nor dread my end." We should learn from this great poet to sweep away our fear of the unknown by having a positive attitude and positive life-long conditioning that eliminates the fear of death.

The mind is our kingdom, and how we use the mind in the face of any bad circumstances is our will. We are the kings. We are each the ruler of the individual kingdom of our mind, which cannot upset us without the consent of our great, royal mind. No one can depress us without our permission. No one can hurt our feelings in any way without the permission of our great, royal mind.

This poem is telling us that we should stop the endless need to conquer the world and prove ourselves, stop measuring our success in all these worldly activities. We should turn inward to the place where there is peace and tranquillity, which is the interior kingdom of the mind. We are only a thought away from Dyer's conclusion to this poem. "My wealth is health and perfect ease."

Another thing to consider in your inner kingdom is to take charge of your health and inner peace and tranquillity. Try to change your thoughts about your feelings, and you will see how the body reacts. With positive thinking, even the body's reaction to illness changes. Our inner kingdom of the mind is quite free. To acquire more, conquer, toil, or lust all produce stress and unhealthy molecules of life, which are catecholamines that can raise the blood pressure, create tension in muscles, cause ulcers, and decrease the strength of the immune system. But positive thinking and a happy state of mind can produce endorphins, which are neuropeptides produced in the brain causing the lowering of blood pressure. These decrease the tension in muscle if a good feeling occurs. Also, they prevent ulcers and strengthen the immune and neural systems. All this occurs with positive thinking. Mind power—the willing of our selves to have positive emotions such as love, compassion, and happy thoughts—produces these endorphins causing a positive change in our minds and in our attitudes.

Put this beautiful piece of poetry in your life. Follow Sir Dyer's suggestion and practice mind control by eliminating self-destructive behaviour. We should catch ourselves in the midst of depression or angry thoughts and try a new way of thinking—positive thinking. Try to put happy thoughts in your mind, thoughts that create tranquillity and peace.

We should repeatedly remind ourselves that no one can make us unhappy. Happiness or unhappiness is all within each one of us; either state is a choice based on what we process in the mind. Without our consent, no one else has the power to make us unhappy. Therefore, we should refuse to allow negative thoughts into our sacred inner space, that is, into the kingdom of our mind. We should not allow these negative emotions or thoughts to pollute our inner space in any way.

In conclusion, remember Sir Edward Dyer's suggestion, "Thus do I live; thus will I die. / Would all did so as well as I!" This you have to remember—that you are the king of your inner kingdom, your inner domain, your inner self. No one else can take that sacred space. If you follow this advice, then you are a winner. You will live a better life compared to those who are not content and toil for an elusive "more." And when you die, you will die in peace.

1. Albert Einstein, quoted in George Sylvester Viereck, "What life means to Einstein," *The Saturday Evening Post*, October 26, 1929.
2. Archimedes on the action of a lever, quoted in Pappus, *Synagoge*, book 8, proposition 10, section 11
3. Edmund Spenser, *The Faerie Queene*, bk. 6, canto 9, st. 30.
4. Aristotle quoted by Will Durant, *The Story of Philosophy: The Lives and Opinions of the World's Greatest Philosophers* (New York: Simon & Schuster, 1926), 87.
5. Henry Ward Beecher (in a letter to his son), quoted in James Samuel Kirtly, *The Young Man and Himself: His Tasks, His Dreams, His Purposes ... His Complete Life* (Kansas City, MO, 1902).
6. Sir Edward Dyer, "My mind to me a kingdom is," in *The Courtly Poets from Raleigh to Montrose*, ed. J. Hannah, (London, Elibron Classics, 1910), 149–150

CHAPTER 6

Mental Discipline

We are what we think. All that we are arises from our thoughts.
With our thoughts, we make our world.
Buddha

Buddha
Achieving genuine happiness may require bringing about this transformation in our thinking. It is not a simple matter. It requires having positive states of mind and eliminating negative states of mind. To cultivate a habit of having a positive state of mind is to exhibit or show kindness or compassion, which leads to better psychological, mental, and physical health. Therefore, the practice of dharma is a constant battle within us; we struggle to replace previous negative conditioning or habituation with new positive thinking and conditioning. The word dharma is derived from Sanskrit, and it means "to hold one back" or "protect one from experiencing suffering and its causes." Through constant training, we can change. We can transform ourselves.

> We know too much and feel too little. At least we feel too little of those creative emotions from which a good life stems.
> *Bertrand Russell*[1]

There are various methods of trying to sustain a calm mind. And, when some disturbing events happen, through repeated practice of these methods, we can get to the point where the negative effects on our mind from these disturbances remain on the surface, like the waves that ripple on the surface of the ocean but do not have much effect deep down. For example, if we receive tragic news, at that moment, we may experience some disturbance within our mind, but it goes away quickly if we have a calm state of mind. If the state of mind is not calm, and if we have negative emotions like anger and hatred, then any tragic news may disturb us for a long period of time. Therefore, it is very important to have the mental discipline to cultivate positive mental states and to identify and eliminate negative mental states.

> Only in men's imagination does every truth find an effective and undeniable existence. Imagination, not invention, is the supreme master of art as of life.
> *Joseph Conrad*[2]

> Whatever we focus on becomes our idea of reality.
> *Anthony Robbins*[3]

Systematic training of the mind is possible by bringing about a genuine inner transformation, by deliberately selecting and focusing on positive mental states, and by challenging the negative mental states. We are born with brains that genetically have some instinctual behavioural patterns, and we are predisposed mentally and emotionally and physically to respond to our environment in a way that enables our survival. By constantly training our mind and receiving positive inputs, as I mentioned, positive states of mind, we can bring about changes to our brain cells: an increase in the neurotransmitters that can bring about pleasure, such as endorphins being released from the nerve terminal endings. By constantly having a positive attitude and a pleasant emotional state, we can increase these neurons as well as these neural transmitters (endorphins). The possibility of reforming the brain's architecture and chemistry has been scientifically proven as well. By mobilizing our thoughts and practicing new ways of thinking, we can reshape our nerve cells and change the way our brain works. The process of reshaping the brain by training the mind is also the basis for the idea that inner transformation begins with learning (new input) and involves the discipline of gradually replacing our negative conditioning with positive conditioning, in other words, forming new neural circuits in our brain. This process can happen with continuous positive thinking and positive conditioning. The training of our mind for happiness is very real and scientifically proven.

> The belief that becomes truth for me … is that which allows me the best use of my strength, the best means of putting my virtues into action.
> *André Gide*[4]

Be more concerned with your character than your reputation. Character is what you really are. Reputation is what people say you are.
John Wooden[5]

---

1. Bertrand Russell, quoted in *A Life Worth Living*, by Mihaly Csikszentmihalyi and Isabella Selega Csikszentmihalyi (Oxford, NY: Oxford University Press, 2006), 140.
2. Joseph Conrad, *A Personal Record: Some Reminiscences* (1912 repr., New York: Cosimo Inc., 2005), 25.
3. Anthony Robbins, *Awaken the Giant Within* (New York: Simon & Schuster, 1992), 160.
4. André Gide, *The Counterfeiters* (1951 repr., New York: Knopf, 1959), 181.
5. John Wooden, *Wooden: A Lifetime of Observations and Reflections on and Off the Court* (New York: McGraw Hill, 1997), 28.

CHAPTER 7

Ethical Discipline

Ethical behaviour is another feature of a kind of inner discipline that leads to a happier existence. Bringing about discipline within one's mind is wholesome when you have positive thinking or positive attitudes towards life in general. Negative emotions and behaviour are unwholesome, whereas positive behaviour is wholesome; the untrained or undisciplined mind generally results in negative or unwholesome behaviour, while a more disciplined mind leads to positive or wholesome behaviour. We have to train our mind towards wholesome deeds to have a happier life. Basically, therefore, negative emotions or unwholesome behaviours usually lead to unhappiness, and positive emotions or wholesome behaviours lead to happiness.

> I grant, that good and evil, reward and punishment, are the only motives to a rational creature, these are the spur and reins, whereby all mankind are set on work and guided.
> *John Locke*[1]

Wholesome deeds are positive. Positive emotions may not come naturally. We may have to consciously train our mind towards them. Traditionally, it is considered the responsibility of religion to prescribe wholesome behaviour, but, to a certain extent in today's society, religion has lost its prestige and influence, and therefore, there is less attention paid to the wholesome way of life in today's society. Human nature is fundamentally gentle and compassionate. However, we must also develop an appreciation and awareness of our gentle nature by changing how we perceive ourselves through learning and understanding. This awareness can have an impact on how we interact with others and how we conduct ourselves in our daily lives.

> If we gather a set of strong enough reasons to change, we can change in a minute, some things we have failed to change for years.
> *Anthony Robbins*[2]

> Words form the thread on which we string our experiences.
> *Aldous Huxley*[3]

Anger and hatred are clearly negative emotions and ultimately lead to suffering. We have to educate ourselves about the harmful effects of anger and hatred in order to eliminate them and to reduce suffering. Anger causes an uncomfortable emotional state in us and suddenly it is easy to feel discomfort when one is angry. Therefore, one has to develop a behaviour in which to avoid anger by encouraging more positive emotions and a wholesome or ethical behaviour, through constantly training our mind that nothing is impossible to learn, as well as trying to avoid all the negative emotions and feelings which lead to anger and suffering. The words we use are very important, and words can be used in a dangerous way to bring out negative emotions in people.

> The German nation is no warlike nation. It is soldierly one, which means it does not want a war but does not fear it. It loves peace, but it also loves its honor and freedom.
> *Adolf Hitler*[4]

Hitler turned his nations' frustrations into hatred for a small group of people through his words. His lust for territory persuaded the German population to go to war. Negative emotions, anger, and hatred can also be conveyed in strong verbal communication, which can change the minds of people. These strong words are actually negative emotions, which lead to anger and hatred, which ultimately leads to suffering.

> If we want to change our lives and shape our destiny, we need to consciously select the words we are going to use, and we need to constantly strive to expand our level of choice.
> *Anthony Robbins*[5]

We also need the ability to judge the long-term and the short-term consequences of our behaviour. For example, overcoming anger can lead to a happier life. Animals may experience anger, but they do not understand that anger is destructive. In human beings, there is a different level of self-awareness: this allows us to reflect and observe that when anger arises, it hurts us and we can also make the judgment that anger is destructive. The more sophisticated our level of education and the more our knowledge about the consequences of our behaviour—such as what causes happiness and what causes suffering—the more effective will be our ways to improve our behaviour in achieving happiness. Therefore I think education and knowledge of how to acquire positive emotions or behaviour is very important to creating a happier life.

> All emotions are pure which gather you and lift you up; that emotion is impure which seizes only one side of your being and so distorts you.
> *Rainer Maria Rilke*[6]

> Without knowing the force of words, it is impossible to know men.
> *Confucius*[7]

> A man's character is his guardian divinity.
> *Heraclitus*[8]

---

1. John Locke, *Some Thoughts Concerning Education in The Works of John Locke in Nine Volumes*. Volume 8 (London: Printed for C & J Rivington, et al., 1824), 40.
2. Anthony Robbins, *Awaken the Giant Within* (New York: Simon & Schuster, 1992), 127.
3. Aldous Huxley, *The Olive Tree and Other Essays* (London: Chatto & Windus, 1936), 82.
4. Adolf Hitler, *My New Order* (New York: Reynal and Hitchcock, 1941), 446.
5. Anthony Robbins, *Awaken the Giant Within* (New York: Simon & Schuster, 1992), 207.
6. Rainer Maria Rilke, quoted in Anthony Robbins, *Awaken the Giant Within* (New York: Simon & Schuster, 1992), 150.
7. Confucius, *Confucius: Confucian Analects, The Great Learning and Doctrine of the Mean*, translated by James Legge (Mineola: Dover Publications, 1971), 354.
8. Heraclitus, quoted in Anthony Robbins, *Awaken the Giant Within* (New York: Simon & Schuster, 1992), 342.

CHAPTER 8

Love and Compassion

We are made to seek happiness, and it is clear that the feelings of love, affection, closeness, and compassion bring happiness. In order to be happy we should have a warm and compassionate state of mind. We all have the potential for compassion and basic human nature is characterized by gentleness. The Buddhist doctrine of the nature of Buddha provides some grounds for the belief that the fundamental nature of all sentient beings is essentially gentle and not aggressive. This philosophy, by its very nature, refers to an underlying essential and subtler nature. According to Buddhist philosophy the basic state of mind present in all human beings is completely untainted by negative emotions or thoughts. There is other evidence that human affection or compassion is not just a religious matter but that we have inherited a gentle human nature. For example, when a baby is born, the mother has the desire to feed her baby milk, and this gentle nature is inherited. As she continues to feed the baby, more compassion, love, and togetherness strengthen the bond in this relationship between a mother and her child.

Our physical health is dependent on a feeling of love and compassion. As we see, a calm, affectionate, wholesome state of mind has beneficial effects on our health and physical well-being. Conversely, feelings of frustration, fear, agitation and anger lead to destruction and to poor physical and emotional health.

> Only those who have learned the power of sincere and selfless contribution experience life's deepest joy: true fulfillment.
> *Anthony Robbins*[1]

Our essential nature is kind and compassionate, and it is the predominant feature of human nature. Anger, violence, and aggression may certainly arise on a secondary or more superficial level. When we are frustrated at not achieving love and affection, there is definitely a tendency towards anger, violence, and aggression.

Looking at human evolution in comparison with that of animals, we see that human intelligence developed as the environment became more complex; there was a greater need for more intelligence and cognitive ability to meet the increasing demands of our complex environment. Since our fundamental human nature is gentleness, intelligence is developed gradually because of our complex environment. If human's intelligence develops in an unbalanced way, without being properly counterbalanced with compassion and love, then it becomes destructive. It is very important to recognize that human conflicts are created by misuse of human intelligence. We can utilize our intelligence to discover and intend to overcome these conflicts. When human intelligence and human goodness are used together, then all human actions become constructive. We should combine a warm heart with knowledge and education, and also we should learn to respect others' views and rights–this then becomes the basis of a spirit of reconciliation that can be used to overcome aggression and resolve conflicts.

> You cannot live a perfect day without doing something for someone who will never be able to repay you.
> *John Wooden*[2]

> Start the day with love. Live the day with love. End the day with love.
> *Richard Carlson*[3]

Carlson's recommendation sounds like a difficult strategy to master, but, if we practice it, it will open up the inner doors to happiness. If any of us could master this strategy to its fullest, we would be among the great models of humanity like Mother Teresa. Yet, as difficult as this strategy would be to master, it is worth every effort. Actually, the wisdom of this strategy is quite simple. The idea is to remind you frequently throughout the day of the importance of living a life of love. Love will become an absolute priority and something magical will happen to your life. Nothing will seem to be more important than love.

"Start the day with love" means that, when you wake up in the morning, you open your heart and remind yourself of your intent to be loving in every aspect of your life. "Live the day with love" means that your choices and actions stem from your decision to be loving, patient, kind, and gentle. "Living the day" means you keep things in perspective and do not take things personally or blow things out of proportion—it means you make allowances for the imperfections of others and of yourself. You make an effort to keep your criticisms and judgments from rising to the surface. "Living the day" with love suggests that whenever possible, you will make an effort to be generous and complimentary, as well as humble and sincere. "End the day with love" means that you take a moment at the close of the day to reflect and be grateful. Perhaps you may say a prayer or do quiet meditation. You might look back on your day and review how closely your goal of "living the love" matched up with your actions and choices.

You do this not to keep score or to be hard on yourself but simply to experience the peace associated with loving and contentment and to see areas where you could act even more loving tomorrow. To feel love and compassion in our lives without expecting any big reward in return will be expressed in unconditional love and compassion for others, which, in turn, will open up the inner door of happiness. If we have this kind of attitude, and we constantly remind ourselves of the benefit of unconditional love and compassion, it will lead to an inner happiness. Striving for inner happiness through love will have an effect on your physical health as well. A happy person is a healthy person. To have inner happiness and peace within yourself and have a heart full of love and compassion will absolutely have good effects on your physical health. I have seen people who are happy, even though they may not appear to be in good physical health. They may be obese, but they are happy. In my experience, I have sent these patients sometimes for coronary angiograms as well, and they have had completely normal coronary arteries and normal blood pressures. The point I am trying to make here is that if you have inner happiness and peace, it will have a positive effect on your physical health.

In my experience, I have noted some of my patients who have a happy personality; they have normal blood pressure, normal lipid profiles, and even normal coronary angiograms.

> If you could only love enough, you could be the most powerful person in the world.
> *Emmet Fox*[4]

Come love everybody with so much compassion that even if we die, we are still alive in their memories.
Smile like flowers, and let your goodwill be like the fragrance of a flower.
Sing like the bird, which sings the songs of love.

Life is that which is full of love.

Come meet everyone with love and hope—that we do not ever separate.

Let the skies look down on you with love, and be happy and appreciative of the joy of love you have endowed on the people you love.

That is the unconditional love with compassion.

Indian poem translated[5]

---

1. Anthony Robbins, Awaken the Giant Within (New York: Simon & Schuster, 1992), 508.

2. John Wooden, They Call Me Coach (New York: McGraw Hill Professional, 2003), 62.

3. Richard Carlson, Don't Sweat the Small Stuff with Your Family: Simple Ways to Keep Daily Responsibilities and Household Chaos from Taking Over Your Life (New York: Hyperion, 1998), 90.

4. Emmet Fox, quoted in Anthony Robbins, Awaken the Giant Within (New York: Simon & Schuster, 1992), 264.

5. The author remembers his father reciting this poem.

CHAPTER 9

Listen to your Heart

He that cannot ask cannot live.
Anonymous proverb[1]

To listen to your heart means that you choose a lifestyle that is true for you and your family. It means that you make important decisions because they resonate with your own feelings, with your own heart, with your own values and not necessarily with those of others. Listening to your heart means that you trust your own instincts rather than choosing your actions based on pressure from others, the expectations of society, or friends, or neighbours or relatives. Listening to your heart, or living from the heart, however, does not mean that you become a rebel and break away from your family, or break family traditions, or become different from everyone else just to be different. It is far softer than that. Living from your heart is about trusting your own quiet voice that emerges when you can be receptive and listen. That quiet voice is the voice that speaks to you from a place of wisdom and common sense, far from the frantic chatter and business of a day-to-day busy life.

> You see things; and you say "Why?" But I dream things that never were, and say "Why not?"
> *George Bernard Shaw*[2]

When you trust your heart rather than your habits, new insights will pop into your mind. These insights can be anything from an idea to move to a different town, to the realization of the necessity to break a destructive habit, or an understanding of how to communicate differently with someone you love. You might also have insights about whom you choose to spend time with, as well as new ways to solve problems. It all starts from listening to your inner self, that is, to your heart.

> Always the beautiful answer who asks a more beautiful question.
> *e e cummings*[3]

Failure to live from the heart creates a great deal of internal conflict, which in turn encourages you to become short tempered, easily bothered, and reactive to even minor distracting situations. Deep down you know what is true for you, what kind of life you want to live, and what type of person you want to be, as well as what type of person you want to live your life with. If your actions are inconsistent with your deeper wisdom, you will feel the frustrations and stresses of life. As you learn to live from your heart, or listen to your heart, the tendency to act in a manner contrary to your inner voice will gradually fade away, and you will become happier, calmer, and less stressed. You will begin to live your life instead of everyone else's life or a life based on others' expectations.

> In a full heart, there is room for everything. In an empty heart, there is room for nothing.
> *Antonio Porchio*[4]

> It is important not to stop questioning. Curiosity has its own reason for existing. One cannot help but be in awe when he contemplates the mysteries of eternity, of life, of the marvelous structure of reality. It is enough if one tries merely to comprehend a little of this mystery every day. Never lose a holy curiosity.
> *Albert Einstein*[5]

To live from your heart or listen to your heart is to commit to yourself and ask the question, "How do I really want to live my life?" "Am I following my own path, or am I doing things simply because it has always been done that way, or because someone else is expecting me to do things the way they do is, or because I am living up to someone else's expectations rather than my own?" Simply quiet down and listen to your heart rather than trying to come up with an answer. See if you can allow the answer to come to you as if the answer comes out of nowhere or out of the blue. You will find that you feel more at peace and you are much happier. The quiet place where you can listen to your heart is a very good place to start. Living from your heart, or listening to your heart, is one of the fundamental foundations of inner peace and personal growth. It will always encourage you to be a kind person; also you will develop a great deal of patience. You should try it. You will be surprised and delighted to know what you will discover—that listening to your heart means a lot, and you will develop a kind of wisdom to understand others and find yourself happier in your day-to-day life.

> You and I have that same power at our disposal every moment of the day. At any moment, the question that we ask ourselves can shape our perception of who we are, what we're capable of, and what we're willing to do achieve our dreams
> *Anthony Robbins*[6]

> The great man is he that does not lose his child's heart.
> *Mencius*[7]

> It is only with the heart that one can see rightly, what is essential is invisible to the eye.
> *Antoine De Saint-Exupery*[8]

> The human body is the best picture of the human soul.
> *L. Wittgenstein*[9]

1. Anonymous proverb quoted in Anthony Robbins, *Awaken the Giant Within* (New York: Simon & Schuster, 1992), 194.
2. George Bernard Shaw, *Back to Methuselah in Bernard Shaw: Complete Plays with Prefaces Vol. 2* (New York: Dodd, Mead & Company, 1963), 7.
3. e e cummings quoted in Christopher Sawyer-Laucanno, *E.E. Cummings: A Biography* (Naperville, Illinois: Sourcebooks, Inc., 2004), 418.
4. Antonio Porchia, quoted in Anthony Robbins, *Awaken the Giant Within* (New York: Simon & Schuster, 1992), 453.
5. Albert Einstein, quoted in Anthony Robbins, *Awaken the Giant Within* (New York: Simon & Schuster, 1992), 185.
6. Anthony Robbins, *Awaken the Giant Within* (New York: Simon & Schuster, 1992), 191.
7. Mencius, in James Legge, *The Chinese Classics* (Hong Kong: Hong Kong University Press, 1970), 322.
8. Antoine De Saint-Exupery, *The Little Prince* (London: Wordsworth Editions Limited, 1995), 82.
9. L. Wittgenstein, quoted in Anthony Robbins, *Awaken the Giant Within* (New York: Simon & Schuster, 1992), 449.

CHAPTER 10

Humility and Simplicity

Happy the man, whose wish and care
A few paternal acres bound,
Content to breathe his native air
On his own ground
...
Thus let me live, unseen, unknown;
Thus unlamented let me die;
Steal from the world, and not a stone
Tell where I lie.
Alexander Pope[1]

Alexander Pope (1688–1744) was an English poet who lived more than three hundred years ago in Windsor on the south side of London. He had tuberculosis and curvature of his spine. He was a short man with a height of only about 4′6″. He suffered from headaches and body aches throughout his life. He wrote this poem, "Ode to Solitude," which indicates the necessity of self-sufficiency, away from the noise of the crowd, away from the big city. We can be content and happy, he suggests, by living very humble lives.

In our century, when the world has become very fast and annoying, this poem of wisdom from a great poet is very applicable. We are constantly exposed to a high level of environmental noise as well as the stress of living in a big city. This exposure leads to an environmental illness. If we follow Pope's advice, then we should take time off, especially if we are living in the city, to go to nature and enjoy tranquillity and solitude. A quiet day in nature can bring balance, peace, and tranquillity into our lives. We should spend extended time in nature listening to the sounds of the birds and animals, and, if we are near an ocean, we should listen to the sound of the ocean's surf and breathe unpolluted air. We know that the wilderness has a great therapeutic effect in rejuvenating our bodies.

The last four lines of his poem impressed me very much—"Thus let me live, unseen, unknown; / Thus unlamented let me die; / Steal from the world, and not a stone / Tell where I lie." I have seen that very wise people have subdued their egos and lived as silent saints. These are the people who do not need any applause from others. They are rich in spirit. That characteristic is truly what is impeccable and magnificent to learn. To live anonymously and resist the temptation to be praised by anyone is truly wonderful. Once we stop needing recognition from others, then we experience the kind of freedom that this great poet searches for: "unlamented, let me die. Steal from the world, and not a stone / Tell where I lie."

This kind of humility can be seen in the great sages and saints of the ages, such as Jesus of Nazareth, Buddha, Prophet Mohammed, and, more recently, Mother Theresa—these wonderful people who lived in this world did not need any praise. They are the ones who let go of their egos and lived as silent sages. At the same time, they have left us great messages—to live a life with humility that brings true contentment and happiness.

There is a remarkable story about Saint Francis of Assisi, the great healer from the 13th century. As he was dying of a very sickly illness, he was asked why he could heal other people but could not heal his own sick body. His response was that he was not the one doing the healing; rather, it was the work of the divine. Such is the humility of great saints who can teach us from hundreds of years ago. To live life with humility and simplicity is the way we, as humans, come closest to the divine.

I remember the words of Henry David Thoreau when he describes solitude, which he sums up in the following way:

> Humility, like darkness, reveals the heavenly light.
> *Henry David Thoreau*[2]

Also, I remember the quotation from a great Chinese teacher—Lao Tzu—who says,

> All streams flow to the ocean because it is lower than they are.
> Humility gives it its power.
> *Lao Tzu*[3]

These great people who have lived on this planet have left us these messages of how to live a life with humility and simplicity, which, in turn, leads us to ultimate contentment and happiness.

Simplicity in today's world involves simplifying one's life by choice rather than out of need. It means we put a ceiling on desires, not necessarily because we have to, but because we want to. We see the wisdom and potential for peace in placing a ceiling on what we want so that we can enjoy what we already have. Simplifying our lives frees up time, money, and energy, so we can have more time for ourselves and for our family.

Many people have found that keeping up with others by continuing to run on the competitive treadmill of life is counterproductive, in addition to being stressful and time consuming. When we fall into this habit of striving after ever increasing wants, needs, and desires, the result is unhappiness. It seems that most of us believe that more is better—more stuff, more things to do, or more experiences and so on and so forth. But, this is not really true. More of anything leads to unhappiness. We get so busy that it prevents us from enjoying our lives. It seems that virtually every minute of every day is scheduled and accounted for, and we usually rush from activity to activity, more interested in what is next than in what we are doing at the present moment. In addition, most of us want bigger apartments, better clothes, nicer cars, and more of everything. Whatever we have, it is not enough. Our appetite for more seems to be insatiable, and this kind of behaviour leads to unhappiness.

Interestingly, the movement towards a slightly simpler life style is not limited to the wealthy. This movement is an understanding, which seems to involve a wide range of people from vastly different economic backgrounds. I know a number of people with very limited incomes who have chosen to embrace this philosophy, and, in every case, they claim it has paid them good dividends. By simplifying our lives, regardless of our status, stage in life, or economic level, we can find happiness. Sometimes, simplifying our lives may involve choosing to live in a smaller, less expensive apartment or house, rather than struggling to pay for a larger one. The decision you make can make your life less stressful because it will be far easier to pay the rent or mortgage on a less expensive house or apartment than a bigger one. Other common decisions, which will make us happy, may involve eating simpler foods or getting rid of excessive things that we have in our houses. It is also important to say no to some of the opportunities we get to do more things.

The idea, of course, is to make decisions that will enhance your life rather than complicating it, in the sense that making life a little easier, a little less complicated, will make life more enjoyable. To be truly happy, we need to live simpler lives, rather than lives consumed by the need to achieve more and more and do more and more things, which, instead, always leads to increased stress and unhappiness.

Buying or leasing simpler cars can save money and possibly trips to your mechanic for repairs. Having few things means fewer things to take care of, and you can take care of the necessary things in a good way, rather than having too many things that you can't take care of in a right way. Every item we purchase on credit is more to pay for. It is also one more bill to pay each month. Having a home with a big yard means spending more time gardening or cutting the lawn, which may not make you happy. Voluntary simplicity is not about giving up everything you own. To the contrary, there are obviously certain things that are necessary or important, things that make our lives easier and simpler. For instance, these days the computer or fax machine and the telephone or car are essential in the North American lifestyle. You have to have the necessities, but even these apparently necessary things should just serve the purpose of making your life simpler rather than more complicated. In fact, without the computer or telephone or car or a decent place to live, life does become difficult. While these things are essential in the North American lifestyle, if we were to go to a village in India or Africa, even these commodities would not be essential. We can be happy there with simpler means. Things like computers or fax machines may not even work in those villages. There may not be enough technology there. Even in those places, people are happy, simply because they have a simple means of living and are leading a simple life.

Voluntary simplicity is not about a single decision, nor is it about voluntary poverty. It is about the decision to keep life simple and happy. We can drive an expensive car, but still we can be committed to simplicity. If we can afford an expensive car, then we can drive an expensive car and enjoy it. Still, how our decisions affect us depends on where we are in this world, both physically and economically. What is more important is the series of conscious decisions we make to improve the quality of our lives. The key is to take an honest look at what is truly important to us in life. If you would like to have a little more time, a little more energy, and a little more peace of mind, it is very important that you explore this matter of a simpler lifestyle, which leads to happiness.

1. Alexander Pope, "Ode to Solitude" in *The Standard Book of British and American Verse,* Edited by Nella Braddy (Garden City, New York: Garden City Publishing Company, Inc., 1932), 182-183.

2. Henry David Thoreau, *Walden, or Life in the Woods in Henry David Thoreau: A Week on the Concord and Merrimack Rivers / Walden; Or, Life in the Woods / The Maine Woods / Cape Cod* (New York: Library Classics of the United States, Inc., 1985), 584.

3. Lao Tzu, quoted in Tom Massey, *Ten Commitments for Men* (Bandon, Oregon: Robert D. Reed Publishers, 2006), 100.

CHAPTER 11

Communication and Shifting Perspective

A Poison Tree
I was angry with my friend:
I told my wrath, my wrath did end.
I was angry with my foe:
I told it not, my wrath did grow.
William Blake[1]

William Blake (1757–1827) was an English poet whose poetry is well known for its mysticism and complex symbolism. He was not just a poet but also an artist, painter, and a visionary mystic who was largely ignored by his contemporaries and considered to be mad. He lived his life in neglect and died in poverty. Today, however, he is thought of as one of the most original and greatest figures in literary and art history. Some of his original engravings are worth millions of dollars.

Communication

"A Poison Tree" is advice from Blake given over 200 years ago, advice for maintaining loving relationships through communication. The main point here is how important it is to communicate.

"I was angry with my friend: / I told my wrath, my wrath did end." This simple message expresses a great truth: when you feel something and you have the common sense and courage to express that feeling to your friends or loved ones, your rage or wrath disappears. But, when you do not communicate, then the anger or rage will increase.

When we are angry with someone, such as a spouse, close family member, or friend, and do not express why we are angry, our emotion becomes like "a poison tree," which will grow in time. But, if we have the courage to express our authentic feelings, regardless of how absurd it may sound to the other person, it is as if by magic or almost instantaneously that the anger subsides.

"I was angry with my foe: / I told it not, my wrath did grow." This is the lesson that we have to learn: if we keep our feelings of anger inside, they will grow like "a poison tree."

I have seen relationships fail because a lot of us keep our wrath inside and do not express anger to our loved ones. By not communicating, we make them our foes. There is no need to play intellectual games with our family members, creating ambivalence and making this scenario even worse for ourselves. The inclination is to keep our wrath within ourselves, unexpressed, which allows us to create, as Blake mentions in his poem, a big poisonous tree. Foolish people water this tree with tears and deceitful smiles. The result is that it will grow and bear poisonous fruit. This tree will literally destroy those who keep their anger inside, if they do not express themselves to their loved ones.

The message from this poem is very profound, and it applies not only in our close personal relationships but also in dealing with everyone in our lives. If we have a spark of anger, which begins to grow, then we should stop and make a person our friend rather than a foe by telling that person whatever it is we are feeling at that period of time. Open up and express feelings from deep down. Be very realistic about your feelings. You have to be honest and use no-nonsense statements. Put aside your anger in an effort to curb the growth of "a poison tree." If you do not, that tree will ultimately grow and destroy you and whomever your foe or enemy is.

In close family relationships, when you feel someone is angry with you, practise the courage to say how you feel without being abusive or loud. You will find that the silent treatment will make the anger grow and not subside. In fact, the anger will grow worse because both parties are growing their own "poison tree" inside them; they have made foes of each other. Sitting down and expressing how you are feeling will generally lead to an open discussion in which both parties can express their deep feelings, and at the end, they will probably hug each other. This kind of reconciliation happens so often in life. If you open up and discuss the wrath, it will end like magic.

In any relationship, the people who often have conflicts are actually those closest to one another, someone's soul mate or very close relative. When you find yourself in a rage, the person you perceive as causing it is your best instructor at that moment in time. That person is teaching you that you have not yet mastered yourself and that you still do not know how to choose peace. He is the one who is pushing the buttons for you to learn. He is your greatest teacher.

The way to have peace is to tell the most important person in your life, that is, your friend, your soul mate, your parent, or your child, exactly how you feel and take the position of being detached. Be honest and watch how your anger disappears. If you are angry with your spouse, don't go to bed still holding your anger or wrath. This will impact the field of energy that you both share and intensify the growth of the "poison tree."

So my suggestion is that, before going to sleep, simply state your feelings and make an effort to show a sign of affection, even if it means losing a fight. It is very important to subdue your ego at this point, and, in time, your soul mate will appreciate your attempts to be honest about your feelings. Doing this will lead to a very harmonious relationship with your soul mate, your spouse, or loved one. It is very important to create an atmosphere of open honesty, particularly in the areas where there are disagreements. You will see that the disagreements will become less if you let go of your ego and have a peaceful, loving, and harmonious relationship with your loved ones. Let not the sprouts from the "poison tree" grow any further.

Shifting Perspective

We all are very unique and see things a little differently from each other. We have our own preferences and needs. Because we are brought up in different ways, and we think in our own particular fashion, we have our own subtle processes of resolving conflicts as well as our own theories as to why things happen. Each of us places a varying degree of significance on what is really relevant and important. We can almost always find fault with someone else's thinking or behaviour. We can usually validate our own versions of reality by focusing on examples that we believe to be true, proving that we are right and others are wrong. In short, the way we see life will always seem justified, logical, and correct to each of us, and the other's point of view will not. The problem is that everyone else has the same assumption—they are right and the other person is wrong.

Our spouses, parents, friends, children, neighbours, and everyone else are equally convinced that their versions of reality are the most accurate. It is absolutely predictable that people in your life will not understand why you don't see things the same way they do, and they will think that, if you did, all would be well and wonderful. Knowing that this is true, why do most of us continue to be frustrated by the fact that we seem to disagree so often with others? Why are we so easily bothered when someone else you know and love expresses a different opinion and viewpoint, and interprets things in a different way than the way you think or believe? The answer to this is very simple. We forget, in a psychological sense, that we each live a unique and separate reality, that the way we interpret life and the events around us is influenced by a variety of factors that are completely distinctive. My childhood and experiences are very different from yours, so my take on life is going to be different too. Any event that annoys me might seem to be completely insignificant to you, and vice versa.

The most important way to become more peaceful and less reactive is to remind yourself that it is all right that you are a little different. You will be rather surprised by this fact of life; you should expect and embrace it rather than becoming upset when someone you like or love disagrees with you. Just say that you are trying to be yourself first. Then, put yourself in the other person's shoes and see whether her or his point of view is right or wrong instead of becoming defensive. When your interpretation of an event is different from someone else's, see if you can be grateful and delighted on those rare occasions when you do see things the same way that the other person does, and, otherwise, try to see matters from that person's point of view or perspective. Your opinion on that particular issue will change, and you will probably agree with the other person if you put yourself in his or her shoes and try to agree rather than disagree.

Trying to see the other person's point of view makes life much simpler and easier. At the same time, you have to show your own viewpoint rather than arguing about that particular point. In this way, you can agree on a similar issue and have a peaceful relationship with that other person. This doesn't mean that your point of view is any less important or correct, but only that you don't have to be frustrated by the fact that others won't always agree with you or see things in the same light. In many instances, you may want to stand firm on your own opinions and values, and that is all right, but you can do this with genuine respect and understanding of the other person's opinion and perspective as well. When you do this, it eliminates a great deal of stress and reduces the number of arguments. In most cases, the person you are disagreeing with will also sense your heartfelt respect and will probably be less reactive and friendlier towards you when you take this kind of approach. In addition, you will incorporate a less reactive attitude into your own interactions with others, and you will find yourself becoming more interested in the opinions of others. This will make you more fun to be around, and people will want you to be their friend rather than confront you. You will bring out the best in others, and you will also allow others to bring the best out in you. In this way, everyone wins.

This is a simple shift of perspective, which helps relationships, marriages, friendships, and family relationship. This shift makes life more fun to live. Just start today and see how this different approach to life is well worth the effort, and it will bring more happiness into your life.

There is a reciprocal relationship between a supple mind and the ability to shift perspective. A supple, flexible mind helps us address our problems from a variety of perspectives, and, conversely, deliberately trying to examine our problems objectively from a variety of perspectives can be seen as a kind of flexibility training for the mind. Even on an evolutionary scale, the species that has been most flexible and most adaptive to environmental changes has survived and thrived. Life today is characterized by sudden, unexpected, and sometimes volatile changes, and a supple mind can help to reconcile the external changes going on all around us. The ability to shift our points of view can also help us integrate all of our internal conflicts, inconsistencies, and ambivalence by cultivating the supple and flexible mind.

With a supple mind, we will become more adaptable, and our relationship to the world will become less characterized by fear. We will develop a more malleable approach to life so that we can maintain our composure even in the most restless and turbulent conditions.

It is through our efforts to achieve a flexible mind that we can reach happiness and nurture the flexibility and the true nature of the human spirit.

The question is, how can we consistently and readily maintain our set of underlying values and yet remain flexible? We have to think this way. First, I am a human being. I want to be happy. I don't want to suffer. Other human beings are like me; they also want to be happy, and they do not want to suffer.

Emphasizing the common ground we share with others rather than the differences results in a feeling of connection with all human beings and leads to our basic belief in the value of compassion and altruism. Using the same approach, we will find it tremendously rewarding simply to take some time to reflect on our own value system and reduce it to its fundamental principles. It is the ability to reduce our value system to its most basic elements and live from that vantage point that allows us a greater freedom and flexibility to deal with the vast array of problems that confront us on a daily basis.

There is a prayer by a Buddhist monk, which impressed me very much. I would like to share it with you:

> Whenever I associate with someone,
> May I think myself the lowest among all
> And hold the other supreme in the depth of my heart. …
>
> When I see beings of wicked nature, pressed by violent sin and affliction,
> May I hold these rare ones dear, as I have found a precious treasure. …
>
> When others, out of envy treat me badly
> With abuse, slander and the like,
> May I suffer the defeat and offer the victory to others. …
>
> If someone whom I have benefited with great hope hurts me very badly,
> May I behold him as my supreme guru. …
>
> May I directly and indirectly, offer benefit and happiness to all my mothers,
> May I secretly take upon myself
> The harm and suffering of the others.
> *Dalai Lama*[2]

This prayer by the Buddhist monk is hard to grasp in today's society. However, if we can at least consider that, by having a supple and flexible mind and having love and compassion in our heart for others, we can make changes in ourselves as we open up the inner circuits of our brain to develop love and compassion for others, then this will ultimately lead to happiness. Seeing things from another person's perspective and shifting our perspective—seeing from another's point of view—we can adapt ourselves if we have a flexible and supple mind. A lot of times when we see things from another's point of view or another's perspective, our arguments with them change. We cultivate a habit of having a flexible and supple mind, which will incorporate the feeling of love and compassion for others—even if they are hurting us in some way.

It is hard in the Western world to have this kind of view point, but I think that, by practicing and developing a compassionate heart and mind and love for others and by seeing things from their perspective and changing ourselves gradually over a period of time, we will open the inner door to happiness, and, ultimately, this will lead us to inner happiness.

The ability to shift our perspective and the capacity to view one's problems from different angles is nurtured by a supple quality of mind. The ultimate benefit of a supple mind is that it will allow us to embrace any difficulty in life, to be fully alive, and to be human.

All of us can develop this suppleness of mind, at least in part, directly through our efforts to stretch our perspective and by our endeavours to try to see things from new viewpoints and new perspectives. The end result is the simultaneous awareness of a bigger picture as well as of our own circumstances. This outlook of a concurrent view of the big world and our own little world can act as a kind of triage, helping us separate what is important in life from what is not.

Developing a flexible approach to living is important not only in helping us to cope with everyday problems but also in that it becomes a cornerstone or the key element of a balanced life. Cultivating a balanced and skilful approach to life, taking care to avoid extremes, becomes a very important factor in conducting one's everyday existence. It is important in all aspects of life. For example, in planting a seedling, in its very early stage, you have to be very skilful and gentle. Too much moisture will destroy it, and too little sunshine will destroy it. Too little or too much of anything will destroy it. In the same way, what we need is a balanced environment for our mind where we can have a healthy mental growth.

This gentle and skilful approach, taking care not to go to extremes, induces a healthy mental and emotional growth. For instance, let's say we find ourselves becoming arrogant, being puffed up by self-importance based on our supposed or actual achievements or qualities. The antidote is to think more of our own problems and suffering, contemplating the unsatisfactory aspects of existence. This will assist us in bringing down the level of our heightened state of mind, bringing us down to earth. Contrarily, if you find that reflecting on the unsatisfactory nature of existence, suffering, and pain makes you feel quite overwhelmed, there is the danger of going too far to the other extreme. In that case, you might become totally discouraged, helpless, and depressed, thinking, "I can't do anything. I am worthless. " Under such circumstances, it is important to be able to have flexibility of mind—to be able to reflect on your own achievements or the progress you have made so far and the other positive qualities that you have. This can uplift your mind and get you out of that discouraged and demoralized state.

So what is required here is a kind of balanced and skilful approach to life. With this approach, we are helping not only our physical and emotional health but also our spiritual health.

> The Buddhist tradition includes many different techniques and practices. It is very important to be skilful in one's application of the various techniques, and we should not go to extremes.... When a man is studying and learning, he does not forget the practices of contemplation and meditation. Similarly, when he is contemplating a given topic, he hasn't forgotten the importance of study and meditation. And when he is meditating, he doesn't forget the importance of learning and contemplation. In other words, he always combines the three. That is a concerted, coordinated, and combined approach. This is very important so that there won't be any imbalances between intellectual learning and practical implementation. Otherwise, there is the danger of too much intellectualization, which will kill the practice, or too much emphasis on the practical implementation without study, which will kill the understanding. There has to be a balance.
> *Dalai Lama*[3]

In other words, in the practice of Karma—a spiritual practice—it is important that, by avoiding extremes and always choosing the middle way, one is not led to a bland, colourless existence. We need to understand the basics of extreme behaviours. For example, the pursuit for material goods, shelter, furniture, clothing, and cars and the attitude of seeking more culminates in the feeling of not having enough—a feeling of discontent. The feeling of discontent, of wanting more and more, doesn't arise from the inherent desirability of the objects we are wanting but rather from our own insecure mental state.

There is a tendency to go to extremes, which is often fuelled by an underlying feeling of discontent. It is important to recognize that, although going to extremes may appear to be appealing or exciting on the surface, it can actually be quite harmful. Therefore, the balanced way of life means having a supple mind and adaptability.

1. William Blake, in Arthur Eastman, *The Norton Anthology of Poetry: Shorter Edition* (New York: W.W. Norton & Company, Inc., 1970), 227.
2. Dalai Lama, *Live in a Better Way: Reflections on Truth, Love and Happiness.* (New York: Penguin Putnam Inc., 1999), 16–19.
3. Dalai Lama, *Healing Anger: The Power of Patience from a Buddhist Perspective* (Ithaca, NY: Snow Lion Publications, 1997), 141.

CHAPTER 12

Judgement and Criticism

A Fable

The mountain and the squirrel
Had a quarrel;
And the former called the latter "Little Prig;"
Bun replied,
"You are doubtless very big;
But all sorts of things and weather
Must be taken in together
To make up a year
And a sphere;
And I think it's no disgrace
To occupy my place.
If I'm not so large as you,
You are not so small as I,
And not half so spry.
I'll not deny you make
A very pretty squirrel track;
Talents differ; all is well and wisely put;
If I cannot carry forests on my back,
Neither can you crack a nut."
Ralph Waldo Emerson[1]

Ralph Waldo Emerson was an American poet, philosopher, and essayist. He was an eternal optimist who believed that nature is a manifestation of spirit. His philosophy emphasized that the spirit of the universe or god exists everywhere. In the above fable, Emerson creates a poetic quarrel between a squirrel and a mountain to present his view about nature. He tells us that divinity exists everywhere if we have the vision to see it. Emerson spoke to a new consciousness in which god exhibits his force in this universe in all shapes and forms. The squirrel, which is a tiny rodent, poses as the invisible god force. So too does the mountain that carries a big forest on its back. Yet the mountain cannot really crack a nut. In this poem, Emerson is also saying that each one of us, regardless of our age, size, or shape, is a divine creation, which has unique opportunities to fulfill our destiny, independent of how others perceive us. Emerson's view—that everything is a manifestation of god—includes all forms of life in any shape. In this chapter on judgment, I would like to share with you an enlightening story that I was very impressed by: "A Promise is a Promise," by Wayne Dyer.[2] This is a true story about a mother and her daughter. The daughter, just before going into a diabetic coma, asked her mother, "You won't leave me, will you mommy?" Her mother, Kaye, replied to her daughter, Edwarda, "I will never leave you, darling. I promise. A promise is a promise." In the following twenty-eight years, Edwarda moved from a stage I coma in which she was catatonic, to a stage IX coma in which she could recognize smiles and voices and cry when she was sad. She would voluntarily close her eyes and sometimes appeared to react to stimuli in the room. But, the most amazing part of the story was that Edwarda had, according to those who visited her over the years, some kind of miraculous healing influence. Everyone felt unconditional love coming from Edwarda, which radiated from her comatose body. Even though Edwarda remained essentially immobile, she still could reach out to others in some miraculous ways. It was very hard to understand how this could be. I think it is very nice of Dr. Wayne Dyer to write this story, "A Promise is a Promise," telling us that even though Edwarda remained in a coma, she still had this life force within her comatose body. It is the same life force that is in everybody, in every mountain and squirrel, a life force that has a mission and a destiny. Edwarda teaches us to be compassionate, and she teaches unconditional love, which is infinite. We don't always have to understand everything: it may be better that we don't understand everything in life. Sometimes life is hard to understand, and I think we should leave it that way. But, it is very important that we do not pass judgment on the normal and the abnormal, because it is all the work of the divine being.

What we have to learn is not to make judgments about the importance of or value of others based on what we have come to assess as normal. But, we should see all things as the unfolding of the divine in every person and in every life form. We have to know that there is no one who is superior, and no one is inferior. Our outer shapes and forms are all a part of the divine's work. We have to see the genius in everyone: just as the mountain cannot crack the nut but can carry a big forest on its back, so a very little creature like a squirrel can crack the nut. In this way, we should make every effort to look for the perfections in others rather than be misled by the appearances of the outer container, that is, our body. We should begin to practise the wisdom that is so well expressed by Dr. Wayne Dyer: "there are many things I do not understand, and I like it that way."[3] We should let go of the judgment that compares others to what has come to be labelled as normal. We must not see people as insignificant. Even those who lie in silence, as Edwarda Bara did, are also a part of the divine's creation. She expressed unconditional love greater than the love expressed by her mother who looked after her for 28 years, around the clock. Her mother would feed her every 2 hours and give her insulin every 4 hours; she raised money to pay all of the expenses and would sleep in a chair every night next to her daughter. But Edwarda also manifested unconditional love, as those who visited her have experienced miraculous healing effects, which radiated from her immobile, comatose body.

Self Criticism

It is very true that many of us engage in a negative habit of putting ourselves down, and we are overly self-critical. For example, we may say, "I am too fat" "I'm no good " or "I do nothing right. " These kinds of statements are damaging, yet we hear them too often.

The problem with putting ourselves down is that, no matter how wonderful we are and how many positive and good qualities we have, we will always find verification if we look at someone who is better than we are. In other words, there is a tendency in all of us to find that which we presume to be true, regardless of what the assumption happens to be, because our thinking almost always tends to be self-validating. For example, if I focus on those five pounds I have gained, I will always notice them as I examine my waistline. I won't admire or appreciate the fact that, overall, I am in excellent health. If we tell ourselves that we hate family reunions, we will tend to look for those aspects that cause us displeasure at family reunions. Instead of enjoying our favourite family member, we will tend to notice Aunt Julie or our brother's annoying tendency to boast and brag, or we will focus on and criticize a member of the family who tends to drink. We won't marvel at the fact that, overall, our family is a group of really nice people.

Therefore, if we put ourselves down or criticize ourselves for any reason whatsoever, it is absolutely predictable that we will find evidence that we are correct, making it equally predictable that we will contribute to decreasing our self-esteem and negative feelings. Putting one's self down also reinforces, rather than corrects, our imperfections by putting unnecessary attention and energy on everything that is wrong rather than on what is right within us.

A very important question to consider is, why would we do this knowing that the only possible result is a more negative outlook, more negative feelings, and less appreciation for the beautiful gift of life we have? Putting ourselves down also makes us sound rather as if we feel like a victim of some kind. People who regularly put themselves down are often seen by others as complainers who lack appreciation for their lives, not to mention the bad example they set for their children, family, and friends.

I hope I am beginning to convince you that putting one's self down is really a bad idea with some rather severe personal consequences. Obviously, everyone has aspects of himself or herself that could be improved upon. For example, one of the many things I would love to do is become far more patient. At times, I feel I am too reactive and easily bothered. In fact, I am certain that this is the case when I am too busy taking hospital calls. This, however, doesn't mean that I should beat myself up or put myself down simply because I acknowledge that I am far from perfect. Doing so would only reinforce this problem and make me feel worse; instead, I could feel better by acknowledging that I have plenty of room for improvement and by trying to be better—making a decision or personal commitment to continue to work towards my goals of having increased patience and tolerance.

That is the best I think I can do to improve my self-image. The more forgiving and patient we are, the easier it is for us to stay on the path of growth and the more likely it is that we will maintain increased patience and tolerance towards others. Eventually we will feel that our self-image improves dramatically.

Finally, don't ever put yourself down in front of others or even in the privacy of your own thoughts. This tendency is a very destructive quality to develop. Eventually, it leads to a very poor self-image. Be easy on yourself, as we know that none of us is ever going to be perfect. There is always room for improvement, so keep working towards a positive attitude by building increased patience and tolerance towards others. Be less critical about yourself.

> A man who suffers before it is necessary suffers more than necessary.
> *Seneca*[4]

---

1. Ralph Waldo Emerson, "A Fable: The Mountain and the Squirrel" in *Poetry of the Seasons*, edited by Mary Isabella Lovejoy (Manchester, NH: Ayer Company Publishers, 1998), 227.
2. Wayne W. Dyer, *Wisdom of the Ages: 60 Days to Enlightenment* (New York: Harper Collins Publishers, Inc., 1998), 123–124.
3. Dyer, *Wisdom of the Ages*, p. 124.
4. Seneca, quoted in Anthony Robbins, *Awaken the Giant Within* (New York: Simon & Schuster, 1992), 53.

CHAPTER 13

Triumph and Expectations

The Six Mistakes of Man

The illusion that personal gain is made up of crushing others.

The tendency to worry about things that cannot be changed or corrected.

Insisting that a thing is impossible because we cannot accomplish it.

Refusing to set aside trivial preferences.

Neglecting development and refinement of the mind, and not acquiring the habit of reading and study.

Attempting to compel others to believe and live as we do.

Marcus Tullius Cicero[1]

Marcus Tullius Cicero was a Roman statesman, great orator, and articulate philosopher who lived two thousand years ago. His words of wisdom can speak to us today; following his words can make us happier.

Cicero was a brilliant orator, statesman, writer, critic, poet, philosopher, and lawyer who lived in the century before the birth of Christ. He was also involved in the conflict between Caesar, Brutus, and Pompeii (and many other historical characters) in ancient Roman history. He had a brilliant and long political career as a writer. However, people who speak the truth are always punished in their lifetimes, but they are rewarded after they are dead. He was executed in 43 BC. His head and hands were displayed on the speaker's platform in Rome.

Marcus Tullius Cicero saw that the "Six Mistakes of Man" were present in ancient Rome. They are repeated here, even 20 centuries later, as we see them all around us. The same mistakes are made, and should be corrected.

The first mistake is "the illusion that personal gain is made up of crushing others." This is a very common problem that we see in today's society. The origin of this mistake comes from one's insecure mind as one tries to crush others and go up the ladder of success. Ultimately, others realize how that "personal gain" was attained, and, eventually, these people lose the success in their lives. A simple example is that, if you want to grow the tallest tree, you have to plant the tree and look after it and water it. You cannot cut down the other trees in the forest so that your tree looks taller or bigger. This applies in our daily lives in business and politics, as well as in our own more personal lives. We have to put our attention on our own lives and see how to improve them. We need to catch ourselves in action when there is a habit of verbally putting down others or crushing them. We must stop ourselves when this happens, and we should become aware of paring down others' platforms and building up our own platforms.

The "tendency to worry about things that cannot be changed or corrected" is another common mistake. First of all, there is no sense worrying about things we have no control over because, if we have no control over something, there is no need to worry about it. Second, it makes no sense to worry about things over which we do have control because, if we do have control, then we can act to make a positive change. The common mistake is that there is always a tendency to worry about things that cannot be changed nor corrected. We have seen this over the centuries. This mistake is very common, which upsets our lives and makes us unhappy. We have to ask ourselves, is there anything that can be done to correct this? Or are we unable to correct it? Then, we should shift gears and work on a new strategy, how to correct or improve the situation.

If we have these two questions clearly in mind, then we will get out of the habit of worrying about problems we cannot control.

The third mistake is "insisting that things are impossible because we cannot accomplish them." When we are confronted with a problem that we cannot solve, the right response would be to investigate this problem and see who could solve it. There is always someone who can see a problem from a different perspective. This person may be able to help you understand and solve the problem at hand. We should not insist that a thing is impossible because we cannot accomplish it. There is always the possibility that some other person out there can do something that we cannot. Take my case. As a physician, if I cannot make a final diagnosis for a patient, I will always refer that patient to a different specialist who has an interest or specialty in that problem. That specialist will help make a final diagnosis and help that patient. I have seen physicians who will not refer to a specialist but try to do everything on their own. They are usually unsuccessful.

The point is that it is impossible to do everything on your own. If you cannot do certain things, there are always others who are there to help. The problem may be in their field of expertise.

The fourth mistake—"refusing to set aside trivial preferences"—is evident, as many of us spend our energy worrying about what others think of us. We have our own labels for others. We consume ourselves in anguish with family, co-workers, or friends. We fill our conversations with talk of ego, with self-importance, which becomes the driving force of our lives. This preference takes centre stage. We have to let go of this tendency of self-imposed ego. We should set aside trivial preferences in order to be happy.

The fifth mistake—"neglecting development and refinement of the mind, and not acquiring the habit of reading and study"—demonstrates that once formal schooling is over, many do not develop the habit of reading and studying for the purpose of improving themselves. Most of our lives can be greatly enriched if we immerse ourselves in reading good books for our own personal enrichment. You will find that reading daily, trying to improve yourself, will result in a richer life experience. This continued studying is particularly gratifying when we know we are doing it out of choice rather than for an assignment or for getting a certificate or diploma. We should give ourselves time to read spiritual books, which are uplifting. This study has a great effect on the mind, which usually will help us understand the problems around us and will ultimately lead us to have happier lives.

The sixth mistake—"attempting to compel others to believe and live as we do"—is the most common mistake we make. Too often we feel victimized by those who impose their views on what we are, what we should be doing, and how we should be living our lives. This imposition creates resentment and tension. No one wants to be told how to live his or her life. The most important trait of highly functioning people is that they have no desire or interest in controlling other peoples' lives. I have seen people who are evolved or highly functioning—instead of attempting to compel others or change what they believe, they do not have any problem accepting others as they are.

There is a quotation from Voltaire, from the end of *Candide*, that is very important: "'All that is very well,' answered Candide, 'but let us cultivate our garden.'"[2] We should cultivate our own garden. We need to let go of our tendency to judge others and let them, too, cultivate their own gardens. We should catch ourselves in the moment of gossiping about how others should be living. We need to rid ourselves of the thought that they should be doing things our way. We should stay involved in our own projects and pursuits in life and not compel ourselves to believe that others have to live as we do.

From the great Roman philosopher Marcus Tullius Cicero, we have these great lessons that can be applied in today's life. Through them, we *can* live a happier life.

Expectations are a part of life, and they are deeply engrained in our minds. However, if we can lessen our expectations about how things are supposed to be and open our heart and accept what is, then we will be on our way to calmer and much happier lives. The truth is that our expectations are responsible for a great deal of stress and anxiety. We expect something to be a certain way, the way we want it to be, and we behave accordingly. If events don't happen the way we expect, we get upset, bothered, disappointed, and unhappy. Since life is rarely exactly the way we would like it to be, or the way we expect it to be, we end up spending a great deal of time feeling let down or disappointed, consistently wishing life were different than it actually is or is going to be. Rather than seeing our own part in the process, we continue to blame life and our circumstances, stresses, and frustrations. Instead, we should be accepting of the way things are now and how they will be in the near future. I am suggesting that we eliminate our preferences or our expectations. I realize there are times when you will want certain things or demand certain standards of behaviour that are suitable for a particular scenario, but lessening your expectations is not the same as lowering your standards. It is entirely possible to have very high standards yet still keep perspective regarding your own expectations, keeping in mind that the goal here is to improve the quality of life and to keep things from taking over life. It is ultimately in our best interest if we can see the importance of letting go of some of our higher expectations of others. That way, you can enjoy more of your life the way it really is rather than struggle with the way you wish it were.

> God grant me the serenity to accept the things I cannot change, the courage to change the things I can, and the wisdom to know the difference.[3]

One of the most important spiritual and practical lessons I have learned is that, without a better wisdom to guide your life, happiness can seem to be elusive, an experience that is going to happen some day rather than something you can experience along the way. If we expect a lot from ourselves and of others around us, and have an ever-increasing list of wants, needs, and preferences that seem to dominate our lives, then I think happiness will be hiding around the corner. In all cases, without a ceiling on one's desires, one cannot be happy. As soon as one desire is fulfilled, then another one magically takes its place. Our needs become insatiable. A typical example of this concerns the home we want to have. We start with an apartment. Then we want a larger apartment. Then the desire is to have a house, then a bigger house, then a mansion. There is no end to it if we continue to have this desire. The desire will ever be unfulfilling.

> Although we'd like to believe it's our intellect that really drives us, in most cases, our emotions—the sensations that we link to our thoughts—are what truly drive us.
> *Anthony Robbins*[4]

Recently, I went to Florida where I visited a friend. When I had been there a few years earlier, my friend had been building a house. It was quite a big house. The houses around it were smaller and older. My expectation at that time was that his house would be the biggest in the neighbourhood. But, on my recent trip, I found that there were other houses, bigger than his, and my friend was not content, that his house did not look as big compared to the others around it. His discontentment was evident in his way of speaking. I told him that the important thing was not having the biggest house in the neighbourhood, which he thought would make him happy, but rather being content with what he had.

> If you are distressed by anything external, the pain is not due to the thing, itself, but to your own estimate of it, and this you have the power to revoke at any moment.
> *Marcus Aurelius*[5]

Such thinking is always in the mind. There is always something bigger and better. If we continue to have big desires, big expectations of others or ourselves, and are not content with what we have, then we will never be happy. The same principle applies to all material things like cars, clothes, equipment, and so on. The habit of always wanting more does not apply only to material goods, however. It also spills over into our expectations, leaving us constantly dissatisfied. For example, you may be lucky enough to have a spouse who is virtually always very punctual. One time, he or she may show up late, and you will feel let down and perhaps give your spouse a hard time rather than saying, "Don't worry. You're almost always on time." Or you give a compliment to your spouse saying, "You cook an excellent meal," rather than wondering why the meal isn't better this time. The point is, expecting a lot from others will lead to unhappiness, while accepting what you have with an open mind will lead to happiness.

When you put a ceiling on your desires, basically, what you are doing is reminding yourself that you can be happy now rather than wanting more and more. This will also remind you of the trap of never-ending desires, and you will be encouraged to focus more on what you have and less on what you want. This positive attitude is the basis of gratitude. Gratitude leads to happiness and contentment. A ceiling is self-imposed, causal, and flexible; it is a non-binding agreement to yourself that you won't spend your life always wanting life to be better and better.

There is absolutely nothing wrong with improving your standard of living, buying a new outfit or a new car, or moving to a larger apartment or a better house. I think it is admirable to do our best and to always attempt to do better. However, there is an enormous distinction between doing your best and always demanding that life be better than it already is; the latter means having a prerequisite that things be different or better before allowing yourself to feel satisfied with your life at the present moment. What I am talking about is a relentless, constant, insidious habit of always wanting more and still wanting more, trying to be a perfectionist, or convincing yourself that you will be happier as a result of these actions. Obviously, only you can determine what is appropriate for you. But I can assure you that every single decision or demand that you make involving a higher quality of life and increased standard of living, or more perfection in your choice of job or on the part of someone else, will be very easy to justify. It will always seem as though one more thing or one more demand will do the trick, will make you happy. You are wrong in believing this. It takes a great deal of wisdom to say, "More is not always better, and more is not going to make me happier. I have more than enough now."

If you practice this kind of attitude, I am confident you will discover a route to contentment that you may never have even considered before. You will still have a wonderful life and all the things you need. However, your life will be far simpler and easier to manage. You will feel far less stressed and pressured. The better life is just around the corner, and you will spend less time thinking about what you want; you will be much more easily satisfied with the simpler things in life. If you try this strategy, it will very likely change your perspective towards life a great deal, and you will be a happier person.

> The secret of success is learning how to use pain and pleasure instead of having pain and pleasure use you. If you do that, you're in control of your life. If you don't, life controls you.
> *Anthony Robbins*[6]

We should never take our significant other or our spouse for granted. Close to 50 per cent of marriages end in divorce, and many of us have a painful and less than satisfying marriage. The reason we all keep making the same mistake is so obvious. We take our partner or spouse for granted. We have high expectations of them. We think our contributions are significant and that our partner is the lucky one who does not contribute as much. Many of us forget to say please and thank you, and some of us never do so at all. We fail to reflect on how lucky we are and on how sad and difficult it would be to live without a partner or spouse. Sometimes, we get very demanding of our spouse, and treat him or her much differently than we would treat a friend. Sometimes we speak of partners with disrespect, or we humiliate them in front of others. Some of us believe we know what our spouse is thinking and then make decisions without consultation. There is also the common mistake of coming to expect certain things like a clean home, or a hot meal, or money to pay the bills, and so on and so forth.

Finally, very few of us really listen to our spouse or share her or his excitement, unless, of course, it matches something that we are interested in. I can go on and on to make this point.

The reverse is also true. Almost nothing makes people feel better than feeling as if they are appreciated and valued. Think how wonderful it was when you first met your significant other for the first time. You expressed your appreciation for everything from a simple compliment to the tiniest gift, card, or gesture of kindness. Each time, you expressed your gratitude, and you never took your new love for granted. Many people believe that it is inevitable that couples will lose their sense of appreciation for one another. I don't believe this. Appreciation is something you have 100 per cent control over. You can choose to be grateful and express your appreciation. The more you do so, the more you will be in the healthy habit of noticing things to be grateful for. It is a self-fulfilling prophecy.

If we constantly appreciate our spouses and express how much they are loved, that appreciation will develop naturally over time, rather than it being used just to please the other person. Trying to express appreciation for simple things that are done will keep our lives happy. I am absolutely sure that the decision not to take each other for granted is one of the major solutions to keeping a good marriage. It is necessary to place fewer expectations on each other, to accept things as they come, and to make adjustments. I am not suggesting that you are the one to make all the adjustments all the time. At the same time, expecting too much from your spouse will lead to an unhappy marriage; it is better to accept whatever has been done, rightly or wrongly, and take it with appreciation. This kind of change in behaviour will help in maintaining a long and happy married life.

> The knowledge of the world is only to be acquired in the world, and not in a closet.
> *Lord Chesterfield*[7]

If you can curb the focus on what you are getting back and focus on what you give, I believe that you will stop making the conscious decision of taking your partner for granted. In time, your spouse will also begin to do the same. It feels good to be grateful.

We can quite easily overlook or simply ignore the negativity or idiosyncrasies of complete strangers, but it is difficult to do the same with our own beloved ones, that is, our children and spouses. It is sad but true that the people we love unconditionally are the people that we have high expectations for. In my case, I have high expectations for my children and my spouse. My wife, who noted that I accept the negativity or idiosyncrasies of our relatives, brought this to my attention. Her observation was very true, and I looked into that. I decided to work in a way so that I can be more accepting of some of the idiosyncrasies of my loved ones.

I am perfectly all right with the fact that most people are not always happy, and I believe I do an excellent job of accepting people exactly as they are. However, I have developed a habit of acting very disappointed in my own children whenever they express an emotion other than happiness. What I have learned from this habit is that I, like most people, have the most demanding expectations of the people whom I love the most. Think about some of the obvious examples we see in our day-to-day life. We are accepting of a little mischief from a neighbour's child, but we sometimes are too harsh on our own children and act in a disappointed way and get frustrated when they don't come up to our expectations. I believe that the most important thing is that we recognize our own tendency to have extremely high expectations for our loved ones. We set out to love them unconditionally, but end up expecting too much of them. In my case, the most helpful thing I did was to practise remembering that people are different in the way they express themselves, including my own children. I needed to respect my children and spouse and their ways of being themselves, in the same way that I have always tried to respect everyone else. This truly works. I believe my children have sensed my sincere desire to become less judgmental and more unconditionally loving. I have felt a similar love coming from each one of them. If you make it a top priority to accept those whom you love the most, you will be richly rewarded by the love you will feel in your family.

---

1. Marcus Tullius Cicero, quoted in Wayne W. Dyer, Wisdom of the Ages: 60 Days to Enlightenment (New York: Harper Collins Publishers, Inc., 1998), 21.
2. Voltaire, Candide, New York: Dover Publications, p.87.
3. Quoted in Wayne W. Dyer, Your Sacred Self: Making the Decision to be Free (Harper Collins Publishers, Inc., 1995), 282.
4. Anthony Robbins, Awaken the Giant Within (New York: Simon & Schuster, 1992), 61.
5. Marcus Aurelius, quoted in Anthony Robbins, Awaken the Giant Within (New York: Simon & Schuster, 1992), 60.
6. Anthony Robbins, Awaken the Giant Within (New York: Simon & Schuster, 1992), 54.
7. Lord Chesterfield, Letters to His Son (London: M. W. Dunne, 1901), 435.

CHAPTER 14

Moods and Expectations

We lift ourselves by our thoughts.
We climb upon our vision of ourselves.
Orison Swett Marden[1]

Moods are one of those mysterious and sometimes annoying facts of life that everyone must deal with. They are unavoidable. However, understanding moods can help you to deflect a large percentage of annoyances, making your life seem smoother and more manageable most of the time. Moods are like internal feelings constantly changing. With our changing moods, come different perceptions of life. Generally speaking, when you are in a good mood, everything seems to look nice. When you are in a good state of mind, life looks pretty darn good! Despite life's imperfections, you feel grateful for your family and for your home. For the most part, you accept your life, whatever it is, and make an effort to make the best of it. Problems don't seem like the end of the world, and solutions seem to present themselves with relative ease. You feel lucky to have a family and a home to live in. You enjoy your children and spouse when you are in a good mood. You are proud of the way you work together and how much you love them. You express these feelings in your home. You take all of your responsibilities in stride and overlook the day-to-day irritations that must be dealt with. If someone criticizes you, you just smile at yourself knowing that the accuser may have a legitimate point. In a nutshell, though, you maintain your perspective and a sense of humour, and you make the best of the incredible gift of life and love.

However, when one is in a bad mood, the exact same life and identical circumstances look drastically different. Everything seems serious and urgent. You have very little patience or tolerance for imperfections. Instead of being grateful for your life, you tend to complain and think about its many imperfections. Although you love your children immensely, you are easily annoyed and bothered by all the attention they require and by the inconvenience of taking care of their numerous small needs. Your home seems more like a bother than a blessing. You notice and think about your spouse's imperfections, and you blame others for the problems around the house. Sometimes even the small things bother you. Or there are no small things! Everything seems to be a big deal, a great burden. In short, you are irritable when you are in a low mood.

> I am not discouraged, because every wrong attempt discarded is another step forward.
> *Thomas Edison*[2]

Moods determine the way we see and experience our lives. As our moods grow and we feel good, we look better. As our moods deteriorate, life seems to look worse and feel difficult. Again, to reinforce how significant moods are, you have to keep in mind how different your life looks, even from one hour to the next, depending upon the kind of mood you are in. Simple as it sounds, learning to detect what mood you are in and to make allowances for the changing of your mood can make an enormous difference in the quality of your life; then you can tone down your reactivity in a very significant way. The most important thing is to accept the fact that changing moods are a fact of life and to understand absolutely the way you are going to experience your low moods. Remember, your mood change affects not only your life but also the lives of those around you as well. Recognizing that the difference you see is just your changing mood can give you a great deal of perspective. You can learn to expect to see things in a positive light when you are feeling good and in a negative light when you are feeling down.

This expectation allows you to take less seriously whatever it is that is bothering you, and you can learn to blame your mood instead of your life, your family, and all your troubles. Keep in mind that if something is truly responsible for the change, it is probably your negative feelings, which you have to overcome.

The truth is the vast majority of things that bother you while you are in a low or down mood are the things you are able to take in stride and strive towards when you are in a good or higher state of mind, a good mood.

In my experience, I was taking too many hospital calls, and, whenever I was on call, I would be in a very low mood; this bad mood was noticed by my family, my friends, and the people I worked with. Even if they did not know I was on call, they would joke by saying, "I think you must be on call today!" From this, I gathered that my expectations of myself were too high, that I would internalize things too much so that I would be in a low mood whenever I was on call. I am an internist and a respirologist, and I do critical medicine (which I have done for the last 15+ years). When I was young, I would take 6 to 10 calls a month without any problem, but after 15 years of critical care calls, I was in a state of mind where I felt burned out and low when I was stressed. It is very important that you know yourself. What is the best for you? Listen to your inner voice. Listen to your body—what is it saying? In my case, I am very compassionate, and I tend to internalize things. I feel bad when one of my patients is dying in the intensive care unit. I would probably not sleep the whole night just thinking about that patient, even though I just could not do anything for him. This stress would affect me in a powerful way. My moods used to be low while I was under the stress of being on call. I did cut down my call schedule quite a bit. I feel that, since then, I have been in a good mood or good state of mind with positive feelings now that I see life in a different perspective.

> Man is not the creature of circumstances; circumstances are the creatures of men.
> *Benjamin Disraeli*[3]

It is very important to remember that moods and expectations of yourself go hand in hand. You have to know yourself to understand what you should expect from yourself. Everyone is different. Sometimes we expect a lot from ourselves and push ourselves to an extreme so that our physical health suffers. For example, in my case, I felt that the high stress work and the patient load of the intensive care unit calls, which had gradually increased over the years, caused my physical health to suffer. My blood pressure was going up, and I felt I had to lower my expectations of myself and do the best I could. If our own mental health and expectations of ourselves are so high that we cannot hear our inner voices, then our physical health suffers.

It is very important to know ourselves, to know how we are feeling, and also to listen to those around us, such as our children or our spouse, and the people we work with. How do they perceive us? A high expectation of yourself when you cannot really fulfil those expectations will definitely put you in a low mood. That will definitely make your life very unhappy. It is very important to know yourself—to know what you can do, to listen to your inner voice, and to have a level of expectation such that you can fulfil your duties at different stages of your life. When you are young, you can do a lot more, but as you grow older, you must bring your expectations to the level of your performance so that you can be happy with yourself. Also, with your lowered expectation of performance, the people around you are happier. The point here is that moods and expectations go hand in hand, and it is very important that your expectations of yourself are at the appropriate level of your abilities so that your moods can be high so that you can enjoy life and be happy.

> Nothing splendid has ever been achieved, except by those who dared to believe that something inside of them was superior to circumstance.
> *Bruce Barton*[4]

We all make sacrifices and trade-offs in our relationships with our family and in our jobs. Most of these sacrifices are well worth it, but, as with most things, too much is still too much. Obviously, the tolerance levels to stress must be adjusted with lack of sleep, sacrifice, hardships, and such things. These levels, also, will vary from person to person. In other words, some things are super easy for some people but may be difficult for another. However, if we can pay attention and be honest about our feelings, each of us knows when the level of stress has risen too high. When it does, we usually feel incredibly frustrated, agitated, and, perhaps most of all, resentful. We may feel a little self-righteous and tell ourselves that we are working harder than others and that we are tougher than others. Many of us have fallen prey to the seduction of having become a self-appointed martyr. It is easy for this to happen. There is often a fine line between working hard out of actual necessity and doing it out of a perceived necessity. The sad truth, however, is that no one actually benefits from becoming a martyr.

> Each of us inevitable,
> Each of us limitless—each of us with his or her right upon earth,
> Each of us allow'd the eternal purports of the earth,
> Each of us here as divinely as any is here.
> *Walt Whitman*[5]

A martyr is his own worse enemy, constantly filling his head with lists of things to do. A martyr is always reminding herself how difficult her life is and how she has to complete so many tasks in a day. This mental anguish takes away the joy of life. People around a martyr feel that he is probably a serious complainer who is too self-absorbed to see the beauty of life. Rather than feeling sorry for the martyr or seeing her as a victim, they experience distaste. The problems of the martyr are completely self-created.

I urge you to avoid this tendency to become a martyr and, rather than spending one hundred per cent of your energy doing things for other people, leave something for someone else to do. If you have time, take up a hobby and spend some time doing something just for yourself and enjoy life. Several things will amaze you. You will actually start to enjoy your life and experience more energy, as you feel less stressed and frustrated. Nothing takes more energy than feeling resentful and victimized by your own self, making yourself a martyr, and having very high expectations of yourself that you cannot fulfil. Second, as you let go of the feelings of resentment and that everything you do you do out of obligation, others will begin to appreciate you more than before. Rather than feeling that you resent them, they will feel as if you enjoy and appreciate them, which you will in the future.

In short, everyone wins and benefits when you give up your attitude of a victim or your tendency to become a martyr. It is necessary to give up the high expectations of yourself that you cannot fulfil in the first place.

---

1. Orison Swett Marden, quoted in Allen W. Janssen, *The Plain Truth about God—101: What the Church Doesn't Want You to Know,* (London, Ontario: Janssen International Publishing, 2002), 192.
2. Thomas Edison, quoted in Larry Chang, *Wisdom for the Soul* (Washington: Gnosophia, 2006), 293.
3. Benjamin Disraeli, quoted Anthony Robbins, *Awaken the Giant Within* (New York: Simon & Schuster, 1992), 33.
4. Bruce Barton, *The Man Nobody Knows* (Indianapolis: Bobbs-Merrill Company, Inc. 1962), 46.
5. Walt Whitman, from "Salut au Monde!" in *Walt Whitman: The Complete Poems* (London: Penguin Books, Ltd., 1996), 177.

CHAPTER 15

To be Human is Divine

> You are a distinct portion of the essence of God in yourself. Why, then, are you ignorant of your noble birth? Why do you not consider whence you came? Why do you not remember, when you are eating, who you are, who eats, and whom you feed? Do you not know that it is the divine you feed, the divine you exercise? You carry a God about with you.
> *Epictetus*[1]

Epictetus was a Greek slave and a great philosopher whose written work has survived through his pupil Arrian. His teachings are essential doctrines in Christian manuals. Epictetus was born as a slave in the first century after the crucifixion and became a free man in 90 AD. Then the Emperor of Rome expelled Epictetus for criticizing the emperor's tyrannical rule. The philosophical insights, which have come down to us from over 2000 years ago, are very important to help us to understand that we humans are divine creations of god. In the section of the quotation in which he says, "You are a distinct portion of the essence of God," Epictetus reminds us of what we often forget: that we have the divine part of god in us.

This great idea, even after 2000 years, is difficult to grasp. But, if we imagine and are aware that we carry god about within us, that god is everywhere, then we can understand that there is no place that god is not. That "everywhere" definitely includes all of us. Once we have this understanding, we gain the power of our source instead of seeing ourselves as being separate from the miraculous power of the divine. We then can claim our divinity and claim all the potency that the divine has in us.

These words of wisdom make great sense: that the idea of god as separate and distinct from ourselves is not true. As Epictetus suggests, we are the principle work of god and a fragment of god.

Sai Baba is an avatar living in India who knows and practises being a divine creation of god. He claims that he has a spark of god in him. He publicly demonstrates his godliness in many ways. When one of the Western journalists asked him, "Are you god?" he very gently responded, "Yes I am, and so are you. The only difference between you and me is that I know it, you don't."[2] When we know we are a divine manifestation of god, then we try to make conscious contact with the divine, and we treat others and ourselves as expressions of god.

We should trust in our divine nature and never dispute our nobility, and also we should treat ourselves with the same reverence as we treat the divine.

> Men are disturbed, not by things that happen, but by their opinion of the things that happen.
> *Epictetus*[3]

It is our opinion of things, and not the things themselves, that causes the disturbances in our lives. This fact is a great source of liberation to know that nothing out there can make us unhappy. We have total control of how we feel and how we process events and opinions of other people. It is in our total control how we process our lives.

There is an ancient Sanskrit saying, "God sleeps in the minerals, awakens in the plants, walks in the animals, and thinks in you." This, in other words, says that there is no place that god, the divine, isn't. God is everywhere. God sleeps in you, awakens in you, and walks in you.

God, the divine, is the universal source of all life, and to feel the power of the divine is to realize the enormity of our thinking capacity. With this understanding, we can more easily refrain from blowing things out of proportion. We should take the circumstances and opinions of others that cause us to feel uneasy and unsettled and use the divine within us as an invisible source to process those extremes that determine our happiness. We should realize that the divine is all around us and can be felt everywhere, particularly in our opinions of things that happen to us.

We should remind ourselves that we are divine creations and entitled to be treated lovingly by others as well as by ourselves. We should let go of our inclination to blame external circumstances for our unhappiness. When we are disturbed about particular circumstances, we should work at them until the brain is calm. This calmness can be accomplished readily if we are willing to shift the blame and proceed to the realization of the divine in us, which, as Epictetus pointed out 2000 years ago, is a means to improve our lives.

One day, I was complaining to a friend about how much responsibility I had when I was doing critical care calls and how difficult my life seemed to be. His response played a major role in my transformation from seeing myself as a victim of circumstances to being a person who, for the most part, truly accepts life as it is. His question was, "Is there some reason that you think you should be exempted from the rest of the human race?" In other words, was there some reason that I should be treated differently from the rest of the human race? He was referring, of course, to a largely overlooked fact that life is full of challenges, obstacles, difficulties, hurdles, and set backs and that most of us are not exempt from these problems. Regardless of your background or race, regardless of what kind of job you have, regardless of your birthplace or parents' background or the money or position you have, you and all of us are part of the human race. It is always easier to see our own problems rather than the problems of others. It is definitely true that some problems appear to be far from severe for us when compared to those of others, but the truth of the matter is that no one's life is particularly easy, at least not all of the time.

There is an old saying, which is very true, that "circumstances do not make the man; they merely reveal him to himself." It is very helpful to remind yourself of this fact of life; the saying puts things into perspective. When we remind ourselves that life wasn't meant to be hassle free or perfect, we are more able to respond to our challenges with respect and grace, rather than being annoyed or reacting to every little thing around us. I doubt very much that any of us will get to the point where we enjoy the inherent hassles of life, but I am certain that we can learn to be more accepting of them. You can imagine that the less you struggle with problems and hassles, the more energy you will have at your disposal to solve those problems. Rather than exacerbating the problems you are dealing with, you will see the bigger picture, including the best possible solutions you have at hand. Reminding yourself of the inevitability of problems won't make your life perfect, but it will put things into a healthier perspective and make life seem a lot less overwhelming. Starting right now, if you can view your current problem in a new light, you will discover that at least these small things can be experienced with serenity and wisdom.

I had been working very hard doing critical care calls and, at the same time, running a full office practice. My schedule was becoming out of control. I did not have a minute to myself for several weeks. At that point, my wife Syeda and my eldest daughter Noreen noticed that I was impatient and irritable. I was feeling overwhelmed. Everyone was upset with me. My office was extremely busy, and my secretary Carolyn would say that I shouldn't do my office work today. I looked so awful to her that she thought I might explode any time! I had been too busy to exercise and felt I was getting out of shape. I was complaining a bit too much about every little thing.

At that point, I realized what Syeda and Carolyn had noted: that it was impossible to be perfect to all people all the time. I had clearly drifted off balance, and it was time to regain my bearings. Often we try to do everything. We work hard, stay organized, try our best to be good to parents, spouses, friends, citizens, and, for me, to patients. I was overdoing it, and, at the same time, I was trying to squeeze exercise into the mix by playing golf and also trying to do my chores at home as much as I could. In addition, I even tried to do some reading.

Sometimes it is too much to handle, and the time comes to let yourself off the hook. You have to remind yourself that you don't have to be perfect or put yourself on a pedestal. If you have been really busy and have no time to get housework done, or office work, and if there are a few calls from your friends that you haven't returned yet, you can say to yourself that all of these things can be put on hold. You feel tired and too overwhelmed. It is best to see if you can wait a day or two to do those chores; take time to be honest about yourself and your feelings. See if you can postpone some of the less urgent chores. In this day and age, when so many of us are trying to be perfect or act like we are superhuman, it is very helpful to let ourselves off the hook.

As simple as it sounds, reminding yourself that you don't have to be perfect is an excellent way to lighten up and take pressure off yourself. In my case, when I gave up some of the critical care calls, even though I am still doing a fraction of the amount of critical care, I felt so much better. I am now able to give myself a break in this manner. My life seemed to come back together very quickly. As I began to relax, my family and friends offered me more compassion, and my work seemed to be interesting once more. Life began to become mellow again. Within a very short period of time, my life was back to normal. In fact, it is better than normal. From time to time, I still need to remind myself of these things; then I rediscover the beauty of the simple message of letting yourself off the hook and remind myself that I am just another human being. Try to be human, and not a martyr.

This strategy arises from the understanding that, when you have what you need in an emotional sense, then you will have plenty left over for other people and their needs. If your goal is to become more relaxed and happy at home, one of the most helpful things you can do is to create an activity that is yours exclusively—just for you to do. For example, my ritual is to get up early in the morning, take a walk, shower, have a cup of tea, and read a chapter or two from a favourite book. Sometimes I meditate or reflect on my life and plan for the day. Obviously, everyone is different. Some people may have time for a little exercise as a routine to create a healthy ritual. Others may not. Today, many of us live at a pace that can only be described as insane or crazy as we deal with the big demands of simply getting by, earning a living, raising a family and attending to our daily responsibilities, and perhaps also taking part in social activities, fitness clubs, charitable organizations, recreational activities, and so on.

We are all trying desperately hard to stay fit and to be good citizens, good parents, and good friends. The problem is that each day there are only 24 hours; there is only so much we can do. We have to remind ourselves that we are only human and can only do so much in a day. There are many contributing factors to this increased pace of life, including technology and higher expectations from others such as our employers, colleagues, and sometimes even from our closest friends as well as our family. Computers, electronics, and other such technology have also made our world seem smaller and faster and have masked our limitation of time. We do everything much quicker than ever before. Unfortunately, this has contributed to a sense of impatience, of wanting to do things immediately, and I have seen people getting annoyed that they have had to wait a few minutes at a fast food restaurant or bothered by their computers if the download takes a few seconds more. We get stressed over traffic and completely lose sight of the fact that we are travelling relatively quickly in a comfortable car.

Indeed, it seems our expectations have increased to the point that we want to do everything at the same time. Nothing is good enough, and we have to do more and more in a short period of time. We forget that we are just simple human beings and can only do so much in the limited time that we have. We all try to do too much and end up frantically rushing around from one thing to the next. We are so hurried that we are easily bored and have the tendency to sweat over the small things. In addition, when we are rushed, we have a sense of insecurity. We are so focused on getting the next activity done, instead of being in the moment. Too often, we are off to the next moment and don't enjoy life as it should be—moment to moment.

There is something magical about having a little space of time between activities and having enough time and a sense of calm. A slower pace is a reward in itself. It is a satisfying experience—to keep a sane pace of life. However, a slower pace does more than keep us sane: it brings us a richness that is impossible to experience when we are rushing around and trying to do too many things. We have to remind ourselves that we are human and can only do so much. By simply becoming aware of your own tendency to speed through life and by having a goal of keeping a sane pace, you will find ways to slow down your life and become calmer with a more stress-free life. You will find that if you can slow down enough, even slightly, the quality of your life will improve in many ways.

Just remember—to be human is divine.

---

1. Epictetus, The Enchiridion, quoted in Wayne W. Dyer, *Wisdom of the Ages: 60 Days to Enlightenment* (New York: Harper Collins Publishers, Inc., 1998), 31.
2. Quoted in Wayne W. Dyer, *Wisdom of the Ages: 60 Days to Enlightenment* (New York: Harper Collins Publishers, Inc., 1998), 32.
3. Epictetus, The Enchiridion, quoted in John Marks Templeton, *Discovering the Laws of Life* (New York: Continuum, 1994), 58.
4. Epictetus, quoted in Brian Tracy, *Million Dollar Habits: Proven Power Practices to Double and Triple Your Income* (Irvine, CA: Entrepreneur Media Inc., 2004), 226.

CHAPTER 16

Balance—Putting Things into Perspective

> Every now and then go away, have a little relaxation, for when you come back to your work your judgment will be surer; since to remain constantly at work will cause you to lose your power of judgment. Go some distance away because the work appears smaller and more of it can be taken in at a glance, and a lack of harmony or proportion is more readily seen.
> *Leonardo da Vinci*[1]

Leonardo da Vinci was an Italian painter, architect, physician, mathematician, sculptor, and scientist. He had one of the greatest intellectual minds of the Renaissance. Leonardo da Vinci, however, was probably a workaholic who never did anything but paint, sculpt, and invent; however, even he gives us this message from 600 years ago—we have to take time for ourselves to have a balanced life.

I have seen highly productive people have a great sense of harmony and balance in their lives. They thoroughly know how to pace themselves and clear their minds of the immediate concerns. They take time off for themselves to have a balanced mind, to be more productive in their lives. As Leonardo da Vinci says, walking away from your immediate concerns or project, if you are stressed out, will give you a new perspective—a way of looking at that project in a new light. You will have the judgment to solve that particular problem. If you see the problem from a distance, it may look like a small point at one glance, then the weakness of that problem will be spotted in an instant. It is remarkable that it is an artist who lived 600 years ago that gives us this great message about how getting away from our stressful lives, seeing problems from a distance, and having a balanced approach to problems sheds a new light and a new perspective on them. This great Renaissance master is telling us to go and relax and not work too hard. Remove yourself from the struggles of day-to-day life. Sometimes you should go to your own natural divine guidance for assistance. Leonardo da Vinci is saying that we should have more relaxation for ourselves. When we come back to our work, our judgment will be clear.

One way to put this message in today's world is to learn how to take a serious problem and plan for conducting ourselves in a proper way but also for allowing improvement in our efficiency. In my own experience as a medical doctor, when I see very sick people in the hospital in the mornings and then listen to the continuous complaints of patients in my office during the afternoon, my mind gets tired. My approach is to go for lunch and quiet myself down in a meditative way. I block off the noises, and then I wake up after 10–15 minutes of meditation, blocking off all negative impulses or emotions, worries, or whatever other problems are going on throughout the day in my life or in the lives of my patients. I come out of this meditative state in a very refreshed manner. This ability to quiet myself has been noted by my secretary, Carolyn. She says, whenever I come back from lunch, "Have you gone through your meditative phase of rejuvenating your mind," and I say, "Yes." Otherwise, I could not do my office work. It is very important that we block off the activities going around us and rejuvenate ourselves with quick meditation—even if it is only for 15–20 minutes. This short time meditating will revitalize the mind as it rejuvenates all of the neural transmitters back to their normal states. Your mind can process better after this rest, and you can have a new look at problems.

In my experience, each patient's problems are important. I have to focus on one patient at a time and one problem of theirs at a time. I must block all negative impulses or emotions, the problems of other patients, and even my own problems so that I have total concentration on the problem at hand. Only then will I be able to diagnose and treat that patient's particular disease to the best of my ability.

I notice that, when we distance ourselves from work and when we are relaxed in our own space, we are inviting divine intervention in our activity. There is a supernatural force that works when we are able to block negative impulses. This can be accomplished by completely taking your problems to a superior source, which will guide you in an undetached way. I am able to detach myself from external noises and go into a meditative state where I find ultimate peace. When I come out of this meditative phase, I feel rejuvenated and ready to work. I can explain this in a scientific way as well. When we are stressed, there is an increase in the catecholamines, causing us to be apprehensive, which, in turn, increases blood pressure and heart rate. If the catecholamine surges continue every day and constantly throughout the day, the week, or a lifetime, then they cause burn out. I see this quite frequently in my profession, especially in my colleagues who work too hard. They have frequent catecholamine surges, which burn them out due to acute stress.

A large number of physicians have some kind of anxiety disorder or depression because they have a high level of anxiety or stress in their own lives and working as physicians. This high level of anxiety disorder can be explained on the basis of acute catecholamine surges leading to acute stress and anxiety, which lead to high tension in the muscles and elevated blood pressure and heart rate. The problem ultimately leads to atherosclerosis, hardening of the arteries, blockages in coronary arteries causing CAD (coronary artery disease), and, finally, to myocardial infarctions. High stress levels also lead to atherosclerosis in other circulatory systems to the brain, kidneys, and other vital organs. This causes the organs to dysfunction. Acute stress from high catecholamine surges can also lead to atheromatous plaque, which can rupture and block the vital organs causing major damage.

It has also been shown that acute stress can cause a decrease in the immune status leading to frequent infections. Acute stress can also cause flare-ups of diabetes, which leads to other problems. Also, acute or chronic stress leads to imbalances in the immune system, which blocks the good impulses that prevent tumours like cancers. Once the balance in our immune system is disturbed, there is an increase in tumour cells or in the incidences of malignancy. This kind of disturbance is common in people who have acute or chronically stressful lives.

It is very important to have balance in life, as Leonardo da Vinci so aptly expressed some 600 years ago. Whenever we are stressed, we should go away and relax. When we come back, our judgment will be surer. If we remain at work constantly, it will cause us to lose our power of judgment. Leonardo da Vinci goes on to say that we should go some distance away because then the work appears smaller. More of the problem can be taken in at a glance. A lack of harmony or proportion is more readily seen. If you see work from a distance, it will look easier to accomplish rather than looking huge and difficult, which happens when you are constantly at your work. Being too close to your work and always at your work will cause disharmony and low productivity.

Leonardo da Vinci, therefore, encourages us to have balance in our lives. This need exists regardless of our pursuits at any level in our lives. By all means, be creative in all activities and enjoy yourself to the utmost. The final outcome is to walk away from an activity when your judgment is not in harmony with your perception of the problem. By doing so, you gain perspective. You will sharpen your creative powers.

Therefore, putting things into perspective means that we should have balance in our lives. What I have seen, which is very common, is that most of us deal with major emergencies very well. However, it is very common that it is the small problems that bother us. I have seen people when they are confronted with big problems such as financial crises, divorce, illness, or a death in the family: they have remarkable courage. They are quite innovative solving these problems. But, when they are faced with niggling difficulties, they get frustrated and bothered by the small daily things in their lives.

So, although most of us somehow get through times of crisis, we are often overwhelmed or easily annoyed, stressed out, or frustrated and bothered by the small, daily things that are a part of everyone's life. Somehow, it is the little things that we struggle with the most. I found it very helpful to remind myself each day how small and trivial most things really are, such as dealing with bills, demanding children, a messy home or a busy schedule, teenage parties or quarrelling with a spouse, getting stuck in a traffic jam, unreturned phone calls, and weeds in the yard. All of these small things bother us. I see most of the things that confront us are small problems and not the serious major emergency or crisis. These small problems are all so much easier to deal with when one has the right perspective. Life can be smoother and more manageable.

We are blessed to live in this world, but it is important to remember that we are only human. Being late getting home from work need not interfere with our gratitude. If our children are bickering, we *could* get upset and let it ruin our day. But, we *should* learn to accept this as a part of life and raising a family. If our homes are not perfectly clean, we could feel defeated, or we can remember how fortunate we are to have a shelter to live in. If we cannot afford the vacation we really want, we could feel victimized and sorry for ourselves, or we can plan a special adventure within our budget. I can go on and on, but the point I am making here is that, if we complain that life isn't perfect and wait for life to accommodate us, we will be disappointed. With fewer demands, we can put things into the right perspective and lighten up. The more we are able to do so, the happier and less stressed we will be, and life becomes pleasurable to live.

To put things into the right perspective, we should also be centred in the quality that brings harmony, equilibrium, and balance into our lives. A person who is well balanced or centred is able to remain calm in the midst of crisis and is able to make wise decisions on an ongoing basis. Being balanced or centred also keeps us from being less bothered or annoyed by the little things, and it assists us in keeping our cool. As the phrase suggests, being balanced keeps us from being thrown off balance by the events and circumstances in our lives. Being more centred or balanced and keeping the right perspective will help us deal with our family, our budget, our homes, and all of the important decisions we make in our day-to-day lives.

The easiest way to learn to be more balanced or centered is to keep our attention on the present moment as much as possible. By paying more attention to our thinking, we can learn to detect when the focus of our attention is too much in the past or too far off into the future. Generally speaking, if we are feeling stressed, our mind will be in either of two places—the past or the future. If you observe how you feel when your mind is somewhere other than here and now, you will notice how stressed you feel and how easily things will bother you. For example, if you are thinking about how busy you are and how many more things you still have to do today and someone asks you a simple question, it seems like a burden to offer a thoughtful and good response. If your focus is on your business, this suggests that your attention is elsewhere. It magnifies your workload and makes everything seem more difficult and demanding.

However, if our attention is more in the moment, it encourages us to do one thing as it arises, instead of focusing on ten things that we still have to do today and trying to accomplish them with scattered attention. You will learn to focus on the one thing that you are actually doing, and then the next one, offering whatever it is your undivided attention. This increased focus allows us to become more efficient, and, as we become more efficient, our life will seem far less stressful. When we live our life moment to moment, giving each moment and every event our full attention, life rarely seems overwhelming. This is because we will be less burdened and distracted by the events of our past as well as the events that will occur in the future.

If we are balanced and centred and someone asks us a question in the midst of our busy day, we will be far more likely to shift gears easily without distress and offer a good response rather than being frantic about taking too much time to give a good response. You will be far more relaxed and at ease if you are balanced and centred.

Being centred or balanced, having the right perspective, will bring a feeling of calm and ease. When we can maintain a sense of well being, even in the midst of chaos and crisis, we will discover that life is much easier to deal with and far more manageable than when our attention is scrambled and frantic. Rather than remembering the hard day we had yesterday or anticipating the difficult day we may have tomorrow, we will be able to make today the best it can possibly be by being balanced, centred, and able to put things in the right perspective.

The payback for becoming less easily bothered is monumental. Our stress level will be reduced, and we will be more accepting of the people and events in our lives. We will have more fun and will become more interested, and, conversely, more interesting to other people. We will be a better role model to our family and friends, and we will be less reactive to small things. We will see our life less as a burden and more as an adventure. We will be less tired and irritated by the small stuff. We will turn our ordinary lives into extraordinary experiences of life.

The way to become less easily bothered is to make it a priority to observe our own reactions to life. Take note of how uptight we can be and how reactive we are to the events and people around us. When we make the effort to do this, make the commitment to become less bothered, especially by the small things, we can make a difference in our lives. By consciously paying attention to our own thinking and reactions, we can bring them to the surface and enable ourselves to make a change. Most of our reactions to life are nothing more than habit and learned behaviour. If we practise being rigid and uptight, that's what we will become. However, the reverse is equally true, especially if we can combine a little humility with the ability to catch ourselves in our reactions. If we have the determination to create change in ourselves, we will certainly be able to do so.

I have seen a great number of people who used to be high strung and easily bothered, who are now relatively relaxed and much more efficient. By becoming less reactive and agitated, we will become happier people. We will have a lot more fun in life.

One more thing—every important person in our lives will notice our positive change and appreciate it a great deal as we become balanced, centred, and able to put things in the right perspective.

> It all comes to this, that nothing great will ever be achieved without great men, and men are great only if they are determined to be so.
> *Charles De Gaulle*[2]

---

1. Leonardo da Vinci, quoted in Larry Chang, *Five Millennia of Prescriptions for Spiritual Healing* (Washington: Gnosophia Publishers, 2006), 549.
2. Charles De Gaulle, *The Edge of the Sword* (London: Faber & Faber, 1960), 117–118.

CHAPTER 17

Go With the Flow of Life

The Moving Finger writes; and having writ,
Moves on: nor all the Piety nor Wit
Shall lure it back to cancel half a Line,
Nor all the tears wash out a word of it.
Omar Khyyám[1]

Omar Khyyám (1048–1142 AD) was an astronomer and scholar who lived in Iran. His poetry and thoughts about good and evil, the spirit, matter, and destiny are very well written. This man, who has sent us this message from a thousand years ago, is so very important in today's life. Omar Khyyám was a most famous poet and astronomer, but, in fact, he was a tent maker. He was one of the most brilliant philosophical storytellers. Omar Khyyám's book, the *Rubáiyát*, contains a lesson that has not diminished in the passing of time. These famous words are so important in today's life. They embrace the subtle truth that escapes many of us.

One of the most common beliefs is that the past is responsible for current situations or conditions in our lives. This is so very untrue. It is an illusion. Often, we assign this reasoning to explain why we cannot be successful today. We insist that, because of all of the problems we faced in the past and the wounds we experienced in our youth, we are bound to these problems. We continue to blame past circumstances for current situations. Therefore, we insist that the reason we cannot move forward is that we are living in the illusion of our past, which makes the driving force of life very weak. Living in the past with old memories, if they have been bad, is an excuse. These excuses are used as a ripple out of the past, causing us to live in the delusion that they are the source of our immobility or failure to move on in today's life. This has very nicely been stated by Omar Khyyám who refers to life as the moving finger: that is, once it writes, what it writes is complete and there is absolutely nothing that we can do to un-write what has already been written. None of our tears will erase a single word that has already been written. No amount of wit, piety, or prayer can change a single word that has already been written. The trail has already been left behind, and you must overcome the tendency to keep reviewing that trail. It is only through the present moments and thoughts of today that you will process your life of today.

As I noted in Chapter 13, a very common saying is "Circumstances do not make the man; they merely reveal him to himself."[2] The tendency to blame our past for current circumstances is very tempting. It is an easy road to take. We can make as many excuses as we want, but accepting the current situation in life at the present moment and not living in the past is the preferred path. I think that parental shortcomings, phobias, addictions, dysfunctional families, bad luck, bad economic conditions, missed opportunities, and even birth order are all glaring at us just below the surface of our lives. And yet, the moving finger has already written the story; nothing can be done to un-write it. This point is very important to understand in overcoming today's circumstances and being happy in our lives.

Omar Khyyám, from a thousand years ago, gives us this simple, commonsense message. The past is over. Not only is it over, but it is not even subject to recall or rephrasing. Furthermore, it is an illusion to believe that the past is what drives us. The moving finger is still attached to our heart and can write anything it chooses, regardless of what was written yesterday. This is our wake up call. Listen to the great words of this man who was just a tent maker. But, he was also a genius in his time, a philosopher, a scholar and an astronomer who, so long ago, wrote this important message.

We cannot live in the past. The past is history. The future is mystery. The present is a gift. We should take this gift of life today and deal with it. Live in the present moment to make your lives happy ones.

Live today. Let go of all attachments of the past. All of the excuses and conditionings of the past must be forgotten. You should make the choice to live right now and not let the past affect you today. You should remove all the blame of past history as a reason for the failures of today. Detach yourself from the past and live today. Let go of the fears that have been a symbol of attachment to the past. Self-pity will not wash away any of the petty things from the past; they are but a gentle reminder that a wounded past is gone. We should bless this great teacher that teaches us from a thousand years ago. The past is gone, and now is the present. The future will be. We have to live today, now, in the present moment in order to be happy.

> The only way to discover the limits of the possible is to go beyond them into the impossible.
> *Arthur C. Clarke*[3]

One of the many ways we find unhappiness is by dwelling on the degree of difference between where we are and where we want to be, or the difference between what is and what we expect or demand. In other words, whenever something is happening such as an embarrassing moment, or if we are faced with an important decision, are we going to struggle and fight with what is actually occurring, or are we going to accept it and deal with it? Acceptance has absolutely nothing to do with apathy or not caring. What it means is that you accept things that are happening or happened with grace, as you are not going to change what has already happened. For instance, if you have a leaky roof or a broken television set or computer, you have to accept the fact that the problem has already happened and not take on guilt and punish yourself for it. In a way, this form of acceptance of what is actually occurring in the moment is one of the ultimate forms of wisdom. It is one of the greatest stress relievers available to humankind.

> Men are wise in proportion, not to their experience but to their capacity for experience.
> *George Bernard Shaw*[4]

Peaceful acceptance is not about giving up or failing to make the necessary changes. Life is full of adjustments, and all of us need to take action to improve our lives and strive towards our goals. But, if something has happened that you don't have any control over, then I do not think there is any point fussing over it and ruining your day. Just take it as it comes and go with the flow of life.

Life is a journey, and there are going to be ongoing issues to deal with and solve every day. So many things we may disapprove of that occur are beyond our control. If this is the case, then why don't we step back for a minute and see the wisdom of taking life as it comes. If you do, your life will be much easier and happier.

> Determination is the wake up call to the human will.
> *Anthony Robbins*[5]

I hope you will go back to read this book again and again and come back to use it as a tool to trigger yourself to find the answers that already lie inside you. Remember that, as you read this book, you don't have to believe or use everything within it. Grab hold of the things you think are useful and put them into action immediately. You will see results very soon.

The purpose of this book is not just to help you make a singular change in your life rather it is meant to be a pivot point that can assist you in taking your entire life to a new level.

> Men, as well as women, are much oftener led by their hearts than by their understandings.
> *Lord Chesterfield*[6]

When we go with the flow of life, we have to pay attention to our feelings first and also pay attention to the feelings of our loved ones, such as our spouse, children, friends, and the people we work with. It is important that you do routine work like house work, cleaning dishes, doing yard work, or attending to short term projects, such as watching your favourite television program, cooking duties, or errands to run. But, it is very important that you pay attention first to your own feelings and to the feelings of others who are close and important to you. Feelings cannot be postponed. They are right here, right there, and right now. When they are present, you have only two choices—you can attend to them now or miss the opportunity and leave the possibility of a potential scar. If you choose to neglect or postpone dealing with the feelings of a loved one, it is as if you lift slightly away from the person with whom you are in love. However, if you attend to the feelings of your loved ones in a loving and respectful manner, you receive the love back in your relationship. While no single episode is likely to have a major effect on your loved ones, there is certainly an accumulative effect that takes place, one way or the other, depending on what you choose to prioritize most—feelings or other things to do in your life.

> Man's mind stretched to a new idea never goes back to its original dimensions.
> *Oliver Wendell Holmes*[7]

When you go with the flow of life with acceptance and pay attention to the feelings of your loved ones, you are the winner. The point I am trying to make here is that we should not get so involved or immersed in our routines or in the lists that we have of routine work, even when this work is important. It is more important that your spouse, your child, your friends, your close relatives, or the people you work with have your undivided attention, and it is generally a good idea to drop what you are doing, within reason, and offer your loving presence. If your loved one desires to tell you a story or your spouse desires to share his or her day or precious moment, these are opportunities to share, connect, and create memories. Your routine work, such as lawn mowing or office work, within reason, can wait. But, there are very few things that are more important, I guarantee, than the feelings of your loved ones; it is very important that you give your undivided attention and listen to them. I found it extremely helpful to keep in mind that feelings should be prioritised over practically everything else. When your loved ones are there, you quickly discover you will have far fewer hurt feelings to contend with, and, moreover, the routine work can be moved around just a little bit. The simple shift in perspective can make a world of difference in the love that is experienced and shared in your surroundings at home and the in place you work. So, before you rush out and do your routine work, check in with your family and see whether a different priority needs to be made. When you pay attention to the feelings of others, you will be a winner, and I think it is very important that you understand the feelings of others and go with the flow of life to make yourself a happier person.

> Go put your creed into your deed.
> *Ralph Waldo Emerson*[8]

In this chapter, I would also like to discuss vacations. Many of us emphasize the importance of our vacations so much that we forget to enjoy the rest of our lives, our day-to-day life and moment-to-moment experiences of life. We plan and look forward to our vacations, sometimes as if they were the only part of our life worth living, and we build up our expectations that our time off work is going to the be the highlight of our year that will make up for all of the hassles and disappointments of our daily lives.

There are several problems with this approach or over-emphasis on vacations. Vacations usually represent only a very tiny percentage of our overall lives. Most people spend probably a week or two, at the most, on a vacation in a year. The rest of the time is business as usual, and, generally, people plan 50 weeks a year longing for the other 2 weeks of vacation; this is a classic example of reverse priorities and an exercise in almost guaranteed frustration. The problem is that, when your primary emphasis is on an upcoming vacation, your mind is removed from the present moment. Instead of being fully engaged here and now and discovering the joy of real living, your focus is on how much better things will be on a vacation and how much more fun you will have later instead of now.

> We are what and where we are because we have first imagined it.
> *Donald Curtis*[9]

Another problem with extremely high expectations for your vacation is that, in many instances, they are unrealistic, which can lead to a great deal of disappointment. I have taken quite a few vacations, and, in my experience, a number of them have been very nice; some of them have been disappointing. I am not suggesting that we should not take a vacation and plan for it, but the point I am trying to make here is that we should live moment to moment and go with the flow of life. Enjoy yourself even when you are not on vacation. In my experience, sometimes, when I have gone on vacation with my family and sometimes with my friends for golf trips, I have been disappointed with the crowded swimming pools, the golf courses, or even sometimes the weather, which did not cooperate. In short, I felt that we really might have had more enjoyment at our home in a small town near Toronto instead of going on a vacation spending so much time and money. This over-emphasis we put on how much we are going to enjoy a vacation can make us feel disappointed, from time to time; it is better to appreciate the time you have on a day-to-day basis and try to be happy and live moment to moment and go with the flow of life.

Please do not misunderstand me. I am not suggesting that there is anything wrong with vacations or that looking forward to them is a big mistake. I am also aware that many vacations (and the majority of my own) are wonderful. I am attempting to alert you to the common mistake people make by making a bigger deal out of their vacation than is really necessary or by over-emphasizing how great somewhere else is going to be instead of remembering how special and terrific their lives are—exactly right now—where they are. I guarantee that, instead of relying on your vacations to be happy, you should learn to be more contented and peaceful wherever you are, with whatever you have, and enjoy every moment of your life. Go with the moment-to-moment happiness as I mentioned in a previous chapter, and go with the flow of life. When you do go on your vacation, it, too, will then be a good experience if you have this kind of open mind and approach of enjoying your life moment to moment and going with the flow of life.

If you are unhappy and stressed the majority of time, it is unrealistic to believe that, once you are on vacation, you will be relaxed and calm. I have seen some of my friends that I have gone on golf vacations with, who are stressed back here; they spend most of their vacation trying to play a good round of golf and trying to make a point with their friends during discussions. People who are stressed or unhappy in their daily lives, for whatever reasons, do not live with the awareness that to be happy and enjoy life, as I mentioned, they need the moment-to-moment happiness that comes with going with the flow of life. So these people usually are not calm or relaxed enough to enjoy their vacations either.

I am just trying to make a point that moment-to-moment happiness is more important than just planning for a great vacation and risking an over-expectation for your vacation. I would like you to go ahead and make vacation plans, and, when you get there, have a great time. But never forget that ordinary life can become quite extraordinary if you remember to be grateful for what you already have and enjoy the small things, which are all around you in your daily life.

Go with the flow of life.

---

1. Omar Khyyám, *Rubáiyát of Omar Khyyám: A Critical Edition*, translated by Edward Fitzgerald (Charlottesville, Virginia: University of Virginia Press, 1997), 194.
2. Epictetus, quoted in Brian Tracy, *Million Dollar Habits: Proven Power Practices to Double and Triple Your Income* (Irvine, CA: Entrepreneur Media Inc., 2004), 226.
3. Arthur C. Clarke, quoted Anthony Robbins, *Awaken the Giant Within* (New York: Simon & Schuster, 1992), 409.
4. George Bernard Shaw, *Man and Superman*, edited by Dan H. Laurence (New York: Penguin Classics, 2000), 261.
5. Anthony Robbins, *Awaken the Giant Within* (New York: Simon & Schuster, 1992), 265.
6. Lord Chesterfield, Letters to his Son (Leipzig: B. Tauchnitz, 1901), 82.
7. Oliver Wendell Holmes, quoted Anthony Robbins, *Awaken the Giant Within* (New York: Simon & Schuster, 1992), 394.
8. Ralph Waldo Emerson, "Ode Sung in the Town Hall" in *The Works of Ralph Waldo Emerson, Vol. III* (London: Macmillan and Co., 1883), 230.
9. Donald Curtis, quoted Anthony Robbins, *Awaken the Giant Within* (New York: Simon & Schuster, 1992), 274.

CHAPTER 18

Your Outer Life is a Reflection of your Inner World

> This is the true joy in life, the being used for a purpose recognized by yourself as a mighty one; the being thoroughly worn out before you are thrown on the scrap heap; the being a force of Nature instead of a feverish selfish little clod of ailments and grievances complaining that the world will not devote itself to making you happy.
> *George Bernard Shaw*[1]

> I am of the opinion that my life belongs to the whole community, and as long as I live it is my privilege to do for it whatsoever I can.
> *George Bernard Shaw*[2]

George Bernard Shaw (1856–1950) was an Irish dramatist, social reformer, lecturer, music critic, theatre critic, and essayist on every subject imaginable. He won, but refused, the Nobel Prize for Literature in 1925 for his play *St. Joan*. He is best remembered for his *Man and Superman* and, of course, for his *Pygmalion*, from which *My Fair Lady* was adapted.

I have taken these passages from Shaw and put them in this chapter, "Your Outer Life is a Reflection of Your Inner World," because we see too often in our lives that a person fits the description of "a feverish, selfish little clod of ailments and grievances, complaining that the world will not devote itself to making ... [him or her] happy." I do see people who enjoy life as if they were a force of nature. These are the people who are doers and live a life that is full and active. They have little patience for those who are just collections "of ailments and grievances" and who are constant complainers and whiners. We see those complainers in our day-to-day lives. These are the people who are not enjoying their lives and life's activities, but they are the true complainers about petty grievances. They are preoccupied with the kinds of activities that are involved in self-absorption. They miss out on the true joys of life. Our outer life is definitely a reflection of our inner world.

This philosophical view of life strategies will help us regain our perspective when it seems as if our life is hectic and out of control. Regaining our perspective can arise from this understanding that our outer world—that is, our environment, the chaos in our lives, and the noise level—is usually a reflection of our inner world. We can achieve a balance if we have a degree of peace and tranquillity, which we experience in our minds. Many people have resistance to this humbling strategy. After all, it is easier to believe that our life is hectic because of our circumstances, responsibilities, and schedules. If you have the humility to admit, however, that you are a true complainer, that your outer life is the way it is because you have taken little control of the outer environment, then you do have the capacity to change your life from inside. But you must have the determination to do so by having a very peaceful and tranquil mind.

This is what George Bernard Shaw is saying, sending a message from more than 100 years ago: if you have a nature of being "a feverish, selfish little clod of ailments and grievances complaining that the world will not devote itself to making you happy," then you will be unhappy. Shaw also very clearly indicates that you have to develop "the true joy of life" by "being used for a purpose, recognized by yourself as the mighty one." You have to "be a force of nature" to bring that peace and tranquillity of mind that will allow you to be happy from inside.

Consider that, if you are nervous, hurried, or disorganized at one level, you will probably find a way to engender activities or items that are also disorganized in whatever you do or wherever you go. The question is, what constitutes a calm mind or a calm life? If you think about it, the answer, while difficult to admit, is very obvious. A calm mind leads to a more peaceful outer life. In other words, if life seems overwhelming, the best place to start your improvement is within your own mind. Perhaps you need a break or a change of pace, or maybe you need a little more time for yourself. Perhaps you need to spend less time doing whatever you are doing and spend more time reading helpful books or even meditating or spending time in prayer, which is helpful to some people. Perhaps you need a good night's sleep or to get up earlier in the morning to create time for yourself alone before dawn, when you can think of this strategy and improve your life. Each person is going to require a different prescription because each of us has different needs and different values. Yet, the very act of simply acknowledging that the root of the problem lies within your inner self and not in the circumstances—can improve your situation because it places the blame where it really belongs, that is, inside each one of us.

If you are feeling overwhelmed or frustrated, my suggestion is to slow down and take a look inwards. If you do, I am certain you will agree that your outer life is a reflection of your inner world. By simply noting this connection, you will be able to take steps that are needed to solve the problem. I see many of my colleagues working hard who are quite disturbed, because they are putting too much pressure on themselves and not knowing their inner selves. Over and over, I see people falling into this self-defeating trap, which usually leads to frustration and dissatisfaction. This frustration puts added pressure on an already pressured life. It is like having a silent critic following you all the time, reminding you that you are not good enough by your own standards when you try to do more than you are capable of. This pressure leads to a disharmonious life.

The better solution is to keep a calm and peaceful mind. Having a calm and peaceful mind will mean that you can give your full attention to the present moment and simply be able to make the decision to do the very best you can in every given situation or circumstance. If you reduce or eliminate the amount of time you spend worrying about a problem and, instead, focus your attention exclusively on this present moment with awareness and a calm and peaceful mind, your outer disharmonious, agitated, overwhelming attitude will calm down. By keeping your focus and attention just on the present moment with a calm mind, you will eliminate stress in your life, and limiting stress will increase your potential for productivity. You will also see an increase in the possibility of finding pleasures and joys in the simplest daily activities of living.

We all are constantly thinking, and it is easy to forget, or at least to lose sight of the fact, that when we are thinking, we become lost in our thoughts, and living becomes automatic. In other words, we are constantly thinking about things and how much we have to do in our day-to-day life or how stressful our lives have become. Perhaps we are thinking of how often we get stuck with a big share of the work, and so on and so forth, without a conscious awareness that we are actively and constantly thinking. For example, if you are having angry thoughts and if you have resentful thoughts, then you will feel resentful. It is very common to have negative thoughts. It is like water rushing down a hill, which flows freely. In the same way, most people have these negative, angry, or resentful thoughts come easily to them. If you have hurried thoughts, then you will not have enough time; the thoughts will be stressful, and then you will feel stressed.

The point I am trying make is that, if you have negative thoughts that are actually more common than positive thoughts, you will become angry, resentful, or stressed. However, we truly have the power to change these negative thoughts. Negative thoughts usually lead to more negative thoughts. Soon we are bothered and annoyed by external noise. We don't realize the extent to which our own thinking has contributed to our mental anguish and pain. When this mental state carries on, generally only two things can happen. One, we will continue to think this way until we begin to experience the painful and stressful effects of these negative thoughts, or two, our train of thought may continue until we are distracted by something that is more urgent to attend to. We have to catch ourselves when we are having negative thoughts. We should say that we are not going along this route again and stop it right away. We should remind ourselves that this kind of negative thinking will drive us crazy and exacerbate the level of stress in our already disturbed lives. When we become aware of our own thinking in this manner, it allows us to nip our frustrations and stresses in the bud, getting these thoughts out of our minds; we become able to get back into the present moment. Being aware helps us to regain our perspective and not allow negative thoughts to make our lives seem even more difficult than they really are. Obviously, the earlier you stop the negative thinking, the easier it will be to get back to a normal track of life.

Stopping negative thinking is a simple technique to practice. It has helped me tremendously. When I catch myself thinking negatively, I just avert my attention to something more positive, such as a game of golf at a good golf course or a day at the beach. Or I might recall a happy memory: a patient whose life I saved when I revived him from a massive myocardial infarction has come to the office and praised me for having pulled him back through the bright tunnel of life. They are very thankful to me and come to tell me that I am the person to whom they owe their lives. There have been a number of patients in my practice who, even after 15 years of practising critical care medicine, come and see me at least once every six months or once a year. Every time they see me, they are so thankful and think they owe their lives to me because I revived them with cardiac resuscitation after a myocardial infarction. That gives me a great feeling.

So, I think of such positive things, which makes me feel good that I have done something good. Although it was stressful for me at the time, it was my duty at the time, and I was happy to be there at that moment when I could help someone. The point I am making here is that thinking of something pleasurable or beautiful that makes you happy, whatever good things you have done in your life, can lead you away from negative thoughts. Start blocking off negative thoughts; these bad thoughts can become a pattern and make your life quite stressful. I am certain that you will agree with me that the outer life is definitely a reflection of the inner life or the inner world. Simply noting this connection will show you the steps you have to take to solve the problems of negative thinking, which leads to a very unhappy life.

> I want to be thoroughly used up when I die, for the harder I work, the more I live. I rejoice in life for its own sake. Life is no "brief candle" to me. It is a sort of splendid torch, which I have got hold of for the moment, and I want to make it burn as brightly as possible before handing it on to the future generations.
>
> *George Bernard Shaw*[3]

This great philosopher conveys to us his great enthusiasm for life. He encourages us to embrace life and let go of grumbling, moaning, and passivity by changing how we choose to perceive life as a whole. He is asking us to rejoice in life, not for material outcomes and rewards but for our own sake. It is very important that, when we hear illegitimate grievances and constant complaining, we do not listen to them and then get ourselves out of this negative energy field, which can pull us down as well.

My habit is to go away if someone is complaining about something, as it is very important that we not be involved and avoid the company of those who have this negative energy, which will pull us down. I simply refuse to stay in the company of people who have these negative emotions and who try to complain bitterly about others. I, myself, have gotten to the point at which I have totally taken out of my vocabulary some of these negative thoughts and emotions such as "fatigued," or "tired," or "making excuses not to deal with a problem. "

We should take the advice of this great philosopher to heart. We should consider ourselves to be "a mighty one" above petty self-importance and complaints; we should view life as "a great torch" that illuminates our existence in a magnificent way. As Shaw said, the true joy of life is being "thoroughly used up" when you die, for the harder you work, the more you live. With Shaw, we should "rejoice in life for its own sake." To me, these great words of wisdom from this great philosopher mean that I should refuse absolutely to think and act in any way that denies me the force of nature for which I have been born—my purpose in life. We should be doers rather than critics, complainers, or explainers. We should speak for ourselves and get into the habit of no longer suffering like fools. We should ignore criticism of any kind.

My favourite quotation of Albert Einstein's is, "Great spirits have all encountered violent opposition from mediocre minds."[4] This should be engraved in our mind and spirit. We should live the way we want to live and burn like a candle or a torch to the fullest. When we have totally burned out, after shining as brightly as possible while living a full life, we should hand the torch on to future generations with a message that each of us has one life to live. Live it to the fullest with great enthusiasm and positive thinking.

---

1. George Bernard Shaw, "Epistle Dedicatory," *Man and Superman*, edited by Dan H. Laurence (New York: Penguin Classics, 2000), 32.
2. George Bernard Shaw, quoted in Archibald Henderson, *George Bernard Shaw; His Life and Works, A Critical Biography* (Whitefish, MT: Kessinger Publishing, 2004), xviii.
3. George Bernard Shaw, quoted in Archibald Henderson, *George Bernard Shaw; His Life and Works, A Critical Biography* (Whitefish, MT: Kessinger Publishing, 2004), 512.
4. Albert Einstein, *Bite-size Einstein: Quotations on Just About Everything from the Greatest Mind of the Twentieth Century* (New York: St. Martin's Press, 1996), 40.

CHAPTER 19

Life is a Treasure, so Treasure it

Because I could not stop for Death —
He kindly stopped for me —
The Carriage held but just Ourselves—
And Immortality.
Emily Dickinson[1]

Emily Dickinson (1830–1886) was an American poet who spent her life in Massachusetts. She wrote close to 2,000 poems. I chose this short poem for this chapter to discuss mortality and immortality and how we should live and treasure life. I believe life is a treasure—and should be treasured. Emily Dickinson wrote about the inner spirit, nature, and humankind. Her poems and philosophy are like those of Walt Whitman, Robert Frost, and Ralph Waldo Emerson.

The awareness of death is a source of great liberation; it is a ticket to eternity, as we stop fearing death when we live every moment of the day to its fullest. We have to train our mind to believe that we are immortally mortal creatures. By that, I mean our bodies are mortal, but our spirit is immortal. We have to train our mind and identify for ourselves that the true awakening of the divine nature in us will occur when we understand that we have an immortal spirit. Through this awakening, we will know the true eternal divine nature that we have within us. We will start to appreciate life in the present moment.

The experience of immortality does not come from educational conditioning or science. This is an idea that arises from the depths of our inner being. When we are simply quiet and meditate, we know immortality is true. Our invisible nature is real, and our bodies will go back to the source, to dust. But, if we have quiet, divine meditation, then we can experience immortality for ourselves.

Emily Dickinson has beautifully portrayed this understanding in this short poem. We should stop and realize that the body we inhabit is made up of nothing more than chemicals, which, through the process we call death, ultimately go back to being dust after fulfilling our destined trail of life. The thought is that, beyond the chemicals or after death comes to the body, each of us is an immortal who is free to ride forever in a carriage with immortality. This thought has been expressed very nicely by Emily Dickinson in her short poem.

If you understand yourself to be immortally mortal, if you know that your physical body is mortal but your inner spirit is immortal, then you should receive death with acceptance and love rather than fear. Remember, you will experience death only once. But, if you fear death, you will die every day and every minute of your life. Use your knowledge of your coming death as a reminder to be fully alive each day. You should do meditation exercises, viewing this world without you and shifting your identity away from your physical body to the immortality that will always be with you. With this kind of meditative exercise, you will ultimately let go of the fear of death. You should always remind yourself that we are here for a purpose and should live life to its fullest without fear and anxiety. When we die, we should remember the last words of Robert Louis Stephenson, "If this is death, it is easier than life." Also, we should remember the final words of Thomas Edison: "It is very beautiful over there."

We have to remember that our bodies are just dust returning to dust, while our spirit remains eternal. With this awareness, you will have peace of mind, knowing of your immortality.

I always tell my family and friends, "Life is a treasure, so treasure it." This saying simply means that life is precious. You are very lucky to be here, on this planet. In fact, I believe that the gratitude I have is one of the most important tools for having a very peaceful life. If you have an appreciation for the life you have, gratitude has a way of putting everything into a proper perspective, helping you to remember that you are alive and thankful. Always appreciate that each of us has only one life to live and that we should treasure this life. Too often, we take this incredible gift of life too much for granted. We rush around as if we will have everything forever. We forget the wisdom to attend to our priorities. We fail to recognize and acknowledge that not only do we have family, friends, a home, possessions, health, and wealth, but life itself.

I think such appreciation puts everything into proper perspective and allows us to be grateful and less uptight and reactive. In fact, I am very grateful that nothing seems to bother me; I think that life is precious, and I should live up to my own expectations and remind myself that life is a treasure. We should connect this appreciation with a feeling of gratitude that we are blessed with this life. The quality of our lives will improve: appreciating the people around us will remind us to be kind, humble, and generous. We should frequently take moments to stop and smell the roses and look around. You will appreciate what you have and appreciate the fact that you are alive. I encourage you to take this strategy to heart and implement it in your life. Remind yourself that life is a treasure. By doing so, you are doing a tremendous service to yourself and to mankind.

When I do critical care medicine, I see people at their sickest; often, these are young people having myocardial infarctions (heart attacks). They are helpless. When they are pulled out of their acute illness by giving them thrombolytic (clot blasting) therapy, they are given a second chance. These people, whom I have seen in my practice, are so appreciative of life. They have seen their lives go by their eyes so quickly, and now they are alive again. The point I am making here is that we all are very mortal creatures. We should appreciate and treasure life. You are not an insect, a little ant, or a little animal whose life is predetermined. That creature lives its life and then dies. We should not take life for granted. We should treasure it. "Live as if it is our last day." "Live to the fullest." I am quoting these sayings that I have heard over the years because they are worth mentioning, especially in this chapter "To Treasure Life. " It is so very important as human beings that we appreciate our lives. Be thankful for each day and every moment. If we have this kind of outlook, then other simple pressures or stresses in our lives will be easier to manage. Look at the bigger picture, the bigger concept—that nothing is difficult, nothing is miserable, nothing is awful. Put things into perspective. Everything is a transient moment and temporary. We all are immortally mortal.

One other point I would like make is that planet earth is a part of the galaxy. We are so little and such small creatures. We are so mortal and so temporary. We have to appreciate life and treasure it. Apart from this planet earth in this large galaxy, there are also so many other galaxies, which we do not know very much about. I was reading in the newspaper that another galaxy has been discovered that is several billion light years away from here. As we look up into the sky, we see many, many stars.

Then, we realize that there is not just this planet and this galaxy but galaxies upon galaxies that we haven't even explored. Some of these planets are a dozen times bigger than earth. The point I am trying to make here is that, as human beings on this planet, we are so small. We have been given this life. Therefore this life should be treasured, and we should treasure every moment we live on this planet.

We have to remind ourselves that, when we die, we are not taking anything with us. Despite this rather obvious observation, many of us fail to live as if this were true. Instead, we spend a huge amount of our time and energy tending and caring for material things as if we were here forever. We are always purchasing life insurance, protecting ourselves, protecting our property and other materialistic things. We become forgetful that we are only here temporarily on this planet. It is incredibly helpful to remind ourselves that we are not taking anything with us. This does not suggest that we should not enjoy the things we have or the things we want to have. Instead, it is a gentle reminder to keep things in perspective. Ask yourself what really is more important in your life. Is it absolutely necessary you have this particular piece of furniture, this particular car, or any other material things you want? What do you really want, and are you taking it with you? I am not implying that we don't need some particular material things. I am just trying to make a point here. We have attached too much importance to material things. We are not going to take anything with us. We are very mortal in our physical selves, but the immortality of our spirit is real. Our physical bodies are temporarily on this earth, but our immortal selves should be treasured, and we should stop bothering ourselves in this life with small, petty things.

I guarantee that someday you will look back on your life, and you will be less interested in how many items and achievements you have accumulated. You will focus on how much you were able to express your love and affection to those around you and how much time you spent with the people you love. By acknowledging this now, you will learn to prioritize your goals and take the time needed to nurture your spirit. It can make the difference between a superficial life and a life of spirituality and substance.

Treasure life. It is the only one you have. Be very appreciative of what you have at the present moment. These are extremely important concepts.

---

[1] Emily Dickinson, "Because I could not stop for Death," in *Final Harvest: Emily Dickenson's Poems*, (Boston: Little, Brown and Company, 1961), 177–178.

CHAPTER 20

Stay Young at Heart with Enthusiasm

A Psalm of Life

Tell me not, in mournful numbers,
"Life is but an empty dream!"
For the soul is dead that slumbers,
And things are not what they seem.

Life is real! Life is earnest!
And the grave is not its goal;
"Dust thou art, to dust returnest."
Was not spoken of the soul.

...

Let us, then be up and doing,
With a heart for any fate;
Still achieving, still pursuing,
Learn to labor and to wait.

Henry Wordsworth Longfellow[1]

Longfellow (1807–1882) was one of the few poets who enjoyed enormous popularity during his lifetime. His poem, "A Psalm of Life," was first published in 1839 in a collection of poetry called *Voices of the Night*, which became enormously popular in America and Europe.

The key word to describe this poem is "enthusiasm." The original Greek meaning of this word is "a god within." Longfellow's "A Psalm of Life" encourages us to have a thoughtful look at the lives given to us and to adopt an enthusiastic and cheerful attitude for all that we have and all that we experience. It is very important that we demonstrate enthusiasm for life and radiate it in every way until it infects all of those around us. We don't have to be like a herd of cattle, doing what we are told to do, but we should have an enthusiastic attitude in us and bring that great feeling of god inside us, which will keep us happy.

Enthusiasm is granted to all of us. All of us have god within us, and we should choose to be in touch with this divinity and display it and not let it remain dormant within ourselves. We should let the inner god come out, and we should live our lives with enthusiasm, which nourishes our spirit.

As a great Greek playwright Aeschylus proclaimed, "When a man is willing and eager, God joins in";[2] that is, enthusiasm spreads the joy of life. There is nothing discouraging about life because, if we have faith in ourselves, then fears subside. We can live our lives with enthusiasm, and, by accepting everything, our doubts will be banished. With enthusiasm, we make the right choice to bring great feelings of love and affection, which can be very infectious to our fellow beings.

Ralph Waldo Emerson also spoke about enthusiasm, noting that "every great and commanding movement in the annals of the world is a triumph of enthusiasm."[3] We should make life a "great commanding movement," one such as Longfellow praised in "A Psalm of Life."

"Let us, then be up and doing, / With a heart for any fate." If you notice people who have this "heart for any fate," they are the ones who pursue their dreams. You see them; they love to laugh, and they get excited over the small things in life. These people never get bored. They see life with appreciation for whatever they have. Their eyes are open with appreciation for everything they see. You never see them complaining. These people are living with enthusiasm. These people have god within them. That is what Longfellow means by saying, "Life is real, life is earnest." We should put these words of wisdom into our lives and live life with an enthusiasm that leads to contentment and happiness.

"The soul is dead that slumbers." Let your soul come alive with excitement and live a life with great enthusiasm, so you can be happy inside.

We should change our minds and become participants in life rather than standing on the sidelines while others take all the action. You should live life with enthusiasm, which will lead to triumph. Then you will experience what Longfellow meant when he reminds us to "be up and doing," whatever we are doing, with great enthusiasm, which leads to success and happiness.

> Except ye be converted, and become as little children, ye shall not enter into the kingdom of heaven.
> *Jesus of Nazareth*[4]

There is an eternal child inside each one of us, an ageless child that become synonymous with heaven, which represents eternity without boundaries. It is the same child Jesus speaks of in telling us that we should be child-like, not childish, and live a life with great enthusiasm, as the word, itself, means—the god within. The ageless child in us is eternal, and it has no judgment or hatred. There is nothing to judge and no one to hate because the child doesn't see just our outer appearances. The eternal child only knows how to look at everyone with love. It gives complete permission, allowing everything to be the unfolding of god in every one of us.

This is what is meant by an ageless child inside us that does not distinguish shape, size, colour, or personality. It knows no distinction between ethnic or cultural variations. Therefore, the ageless child is always at peace. It witnesses, observes, and just allows. The ageless child to whom Jesus refers to is non-judgmental, accepting, and loving being, one not capable of placing labels on others. We should realize that, in every adult, there is a child who desperately wants to come out. It is this child who is full, and the adult who is usually empty. The fullness of a child is radiant from the peaceful, loving, non-judgmental, and allowing nature that it has. The emptiness in an adult reveals itself through anxiety, fear, and judgment. The child is, in fact, enlightened. In the heart of a child, there is purity and a pure, divine love and acceptance. That child-like purity is the ticket to heaven.

Therefore, we should make our goal in life to be child-like in everything we do—to tackle all with great enthusiasm, which leads to ultimate contentment and happiness. We should see the genius that is the inquisitiveness of children. Children are always willing to share, to explore, without fear of criticism. And they do not blame. The key word in this passage from Jesus of Nazareth is "converted"; that is, turned away from judgment and towards a child-like love, which is perfect, kind, unconditional, and, above all, eternal. The god within us resides in each one of us and cannot age or die. When we become child-like and leave behind the childish attitude of an adult, this helps us to enter the eternal kingdom of heaven. That kingdom is available to all of us here, now, on this planet earth. I think it is here we reap and do, and pay for our mistakes. Here on this earth, we can make our heaven by being child-like, as Jesus Christ said.

> Man is most nearly himself when he achieves the seriousness of a child at play.
> *Heraclitus*[5]

Heraclitus said very clearly that we should be more child-like, loving, playful, tolerant, and inquisitive. When we are serious, we must remind ourselves that there is an invisible observer inside us that recognizes our sombre side. This observer will quickly be a child-like witness that is not at all like what it is witnessing. Therefore, we must make an immediate change in ourselves to be child-like. Make the decision that you will never be too serious, that your body is rented by this aging, eternal, child-like observer, who is innocent and ready to enter the kingdom of heaven, the ultimate place of peace and love. This kingdom of heaven is on this planet earth, if we see it that way, where we can be content and happy with a child-like attitude.

Stay Young At Heart

Staying young at heart and being playful are very joyful qualities. They keep you smiling and laughing and remind you not to take yourself or the other members of your family too seriously. Being young at heart and playful keeps you light hearted and relaxed, allowing you to keep your heart open to those around you and to bounce back from setbacks. This quality also removes much of the defensiveness that tends to occur around us in our families and workplaces. It allows us to be playful and kid around with one another when it is appropriate. It also helps us to stay connected by having heart-to-heart talks with our family members and the people with whom we work, so we can keep things in order.

It makes me sad to see people who lose their sense of being young at heart or playful. They seem to be quite serious. They tend to be upset and treat virtually every situation as an emergency. These serious people often have a frown on their forehead and a look of disapproval. They seldom enjoy the simple things in life. Needless to say, these people are not young hearted or playful, and they are constantly worrying about the small things in life.

Being young at heart and playful means many things, from the ability to truly laugh at even yourself to being open to all new things that life has to offer. This quality can even mean rolling around and playing with your children, playing silly games or joking with your spouse, and being playful by telling silly jokes at home.

If you have lost your sense of being young at heart and playful, don't worry. It is very easy to get these feelings back. Just start smiling. I assure you, when you start this little exercise of a simple smile, you will observe how other people react to you. If you also observe the people around you who are young at heart and playful, rather than dismissing their behaviour as simple-mindedness and thinking of them as silly, you will soon recognize them as being light hearted and playful. In fact, these playful people are the people who are happy. You will find that they have a very healing and refreshing attitude towards life. Being light hearted, young at heart, or playful is very innocent and fits with our human nature. As you observe others who are genuinely young at heart, light-hearted, or playful, you will notice that they are happy and know how to bring out the best in others.

If you want to be light-hearted or young at heart yourself, you don't have to change your essential personality. Just take small steps towards playfulness, and you can become a little less serious about routine things. You will be very well received by virtually everyone you meet. In fact, you will notice that the company you are keeping will really enjoy being with you. In addition, and perhaps most important, you will find yourself becoming easygoing and even philosophical about life.

One other quality of being playful and light-hearted that should be nurtured and developed is the quality of speaking softly. This use of a quiet voice has a nurturing and calming effect on others. Some people believe that you are born with this quality of a soft voice and speaking quietly. To some degree, this is true. However, in these recent years, I have discovered that speaking softly is a quality that one can also develop. The rewards are tremendous if you nurture this quality. Using a quiet voice will have a positive effect on your family, at home, and also in your workplace.

When we speak in a loud voice, or quickly, the energy we send out into this world can signal the frantic or nervous attitude that we are experiencing. Although our intentions may be different, the people around us will feel pressured or agitated, which can, in turn, unconsciously encourage them to act hyper and irritable themselves. In other words, our voice can perpetuate the cycle of nervous energy, and it carries a great deal of power and authority. It sends a message to those around us of irritability and nervousness. So, if you speak loudly, you send a message of impatience and agitation. Even without realizing it, you and your listeners feel a lessening of calmness, of love, and respect in the home and at the workplace.

> Realize now the power that your words command if you simply choose them wisely.
> *Anthony Robbins*[6]

I am not suggesting that you change your style of speaking. Every individual has a different temperament and a unique style of communication. I am not suggesting that you completely transform the way you communicate. What I am proposing here is simply that you try to become a little more conscious about how your voice is being received by others around you and develop the quality of speaking softly. If you do these things, you will go a long way. Furthermore, I am suggesting that if you make a conscious effort to speak softly, you may discover an almost instant and surprising change in the feelings of the people around you—at home and in your workplace.

> A powerful agent is the right word.... Whenever we come upon one of those intensely right words in a book or newspaper the resulting effect is physical as well as spiritual, and electrically prompt.
> *Mark Twain*[7]

If you have a young and playful nature and a soft-spoken voice, you will feel calmer and less stressed. You will find that, if you quiet down your voice and have a playful nature, this will naturally have a relaxing effect on your body and on your mind. You will also discover that, if you quiet down, those around you will quickly follow suit. Later, you will find the benefits of this little magic; it will come as a welcome relief that you now have a calm atmosphere at home and at work. Often, calming down starts with a quiet voice; this, in turn, leads to calmer feelings and behaviour. If you think about it, this view makes sense. If we want others to behave in a relatively calm manner, the worst thing we can do is yell or act out or speak loudly. The truth is, if we really want someone to listen to us, the best things we can possibly do is to speak with a soft voice and have a light-hearted nature. You will be surprised to see how attentive and respectful your audience will be if you behave in a light-hearted manner and speak softly.

The words you habitually choose also affect how you communicate with yourself and therefore what you experience.
Anthony Robbins[8]

My suggestion is for you to make an honest attempt to have a light-hearted nature and a soft voice. You will be pleasantly surprised to see the calming effect at home and at work, and the respect you will receive from those around you.

---

1. Henry Wordsworth Longfellow, "A Psalm of Life: What the Heart of a Young Man Said to the Psalmist," in Laura Berquist, *The Harp and the Laurel Wreath: Poetry and Dictation for the Classical Curriculum* (San Francisco: Ignatius Press, 1999), 184–185.
2. Aeschylus, quoted in Linda Noble Topf and Hal Zina Bennett, *You Are Not Your Illness: Seven Principles for Meeting the Challenge* (New York: Simon and Schuster Inc., 1995), 68.
3. Ralph Waldo Emerson, "Man the Reformer: A lecture read before the Mechanics' Apprentices' Library Association, Boston, January 25, 1841," *Essays and Lectures* (New York, Library of America, 1983), 147.
4. Jesus of Nazareth, Matthew 18:3.
5. Heraclitus, quoted in Wayne W. Dyer, *Wisdom of the Ages: 60 Days to Enlightenment* (New York: Harper Collins Publishers, Inc., 1998), 29.
6. Anthony Robbins, *Awaken the Giant Within* (New York: Simon & Schuster, 1992), 201.
7. Mark Twain, *What is Man and Other Essays* (Fairfield, IA: First World Library—Literary Society, 2004), 232.
8. Anthony Robbins, *Awaken the Giant Within* (New York: Simon & Schuster, 1992), 201.

CHAPTER 21

Solitude and Peace

Solitude

Laugh, and the world laughs with you;
 Weep, and you weep alone.
For the sad old earth must borrow its mirth,
 But has trouble enough of its own.
Sing, and the hills will answer;
 Sigh, it is lost on the air.
The echoes bound to a joyful sound,
 But shrink from voicing care.

Rejoice, and men will seek you;
 Grieve, and they turn and go.
They want full measure of all your pleasure,
 But they do not need your woe.
Be glad, and your friends are many;
 Be sad, and you lose them all.
There are none to decline your nectar'd wine,
 But alone you must drink life's gall.

Feast, and your halls are crowded;
 Fast, and the world goes by.
Succeed and give, and it helps you live,
 But no man can help you die.
There is room in the halls of pleasure
 For a long and lordly train,
But one by one, we must all file on
 Through the narrow aisles of pain.

Ella Wheeler Wilcox[1]

Ella Wheeler Wilcox (1850–1919) was an American poet born in Wisconsin. Her readers loved her poetry, which is laden with spiritualism and mysticism.

The poem, "Solitude," tells us what our attitude should be towards life. She tells us how the energy field works around us. Essentially, the field of energy is an invisible, vibrant field that surrounds all objects, including us. Others can feel or are affected by this field of energy at a certain level of consciousness along a continuum. If we are in the proximity of people with positive fields of energy, we get that positive feeling in us as well. This field of energy is created by how we think and process our experiences. We feel that strong, continuous energy for an extended period, even when the people are gone, especially when we are in the positive fields of energy. This joyous energy is also felt in places where there are highly advanced spiritual people and where they have lived. Even after they are dead, their fields of energy are present and can be felt in those holy places. Highly evolved people have very positive energy fields that attract thousands of people. The power of these positive fields of energy to attract thousands of people is well documented in the histories of spiritual leaders such as Jesus Christ, the Prophet Mohammed and, more recently, Mahatma Gandhi and Mother Theresa. Even though they are dead and gone and lived on this earth years ago, they have left this very positive field of energy, and their messages can still be felt by millions of people.

The first line of Ella Wheeler Wilcox's poem, says, "Laugh, and the world laughs with you, / Weep and you weep alone." This is a very important message: if we laugh, we create a very positive field of energy, which can be felt by others who enter this field. They, too, will be happy with you. But, if you weep, you weep alone because you create a negative field of energy that no one is attracted to.

I have travelled extensively in India, North America, and Europe. Wherever I went, from the very poorest conditions to the very richest places, I met people from all walks of life, and the only thing I can say is that, when I had, in myself, a very positive field of energy with happiness, I attracted people of all kinds, whether rich or poor. I got positive vibrations from them whenever I gave out positive energy in my behaviour. This message is what Ella Wheeler Wilcox said nearly a century ago: when we have a positive attitude, we have a positive field of energy, and those around us laugh with us. But, if you have a negative field of energy, no one wants to be in our company.

"Rejoice, and the men will seek you; / Grieve, and they turn and go."

This, too, is the same great message from this poet. "Be glad, and your friends are many; / Be sad, and you lose them all. / There are none to decline your nectar'd wine, / But alone you must drink life's gall." This truly indicates how we are attracted to positive energy and reject negative energy in our lives. We are able, within ourselves, to create positive fields of energy to bring happiness into our lives.

I usually decline to be in the company of people who have negative fields of energy, as they will bring me down with their negative force. We can try to uplift them with our own positive energy, but, if there is extreme negativity around a person, excuse yourself and leave that negative field of energy. Another person's negative energy brings thoughts of displeasure and disgust. We should also remember that we attract what we project; in other words, if we give out negative energy, that is what we get back from others, but if we project positive energy, others show us their positive natures. In general, those who feel that the world is beautiful and those who have the humility to appreciate it are the people who are happy. Those who believe that the world is poisonous and do not believe in the goodness of humanity are the ones who suffer. It is all how we perceive things around us. It is all within us—how to project happiness and create positive fields of energy to extend to our fellow creatures.

I usually refuse to contaminate my field of energy by thoughts of displeasure and disgust. It is very easy to give in to negative thoughts, which are like a stream of water flowing down a hill, creating additional negative fields. Whenever we are stressed, we get these negative thoughts creating negative fields of energy. We must stop right there and say, "We are thinking that way again," and, instead, invite positive thoughts of pleasure, which brings happiness into our lives and creates a positive field of energy around us.

"Succeed, and it helps you live, but no man can help you die." It is very true that, when we are successful, it helps us to live a long and happy life. But, if we have a very negative attitude and a not very generous nature, then there is no one who can help us in any way. If you are like this, you will die a lonely death. "There is a room in the halls of pleasure / For a long and lordly train, / But one by one we must all file on / Through the narrow aisles of pain." This passage is, again, telling us how to be positive. "Be glad and your friends will be many; / Be sad, and you will lose them all." This is another very well-expressed quotation by this well-known poet, indicating that our field of energy radiates whatever vibration or frequency we generate, and if we are impacting and being impacted by the energy fields of many people who are negative and refuse to give, then these are the people who opt for weeping rather than laughing. They opt for grieving rather than rejoicing. These are the people who opt for sighing rather than singing. These are the people who bring sadness rather than gladness. These negative attitudes produce negative fields of energy, which produce pain rather than pleasure. These unhappy people pollute their own mental energy fields so much that they bring total unhappiness to themselves and to the people around them. "Weep, and you weep alone" is a very well-written line in this great poem. You should be happy and have a positive field of energy around you. That way, those around you will laugh with you. We should lighten up and take ourselves less seriously. Detach yourself from self-importance: that will bring happiness into your life.

We should smile in difficult situations as frowning radiates negativity. Cheer instead of criticize. We have total control over how much we laugh, rejoice, and sing, regardless of how much we convince ourselves of the contrary. Therefore, when we enter negative fields, we need to consciously make an effort to deflect the negative energy by being positive, with a smile on our face when others are frowning. We need to radiate happiness and cheer when we are faced with criticism and negativity.

To have a peaceful nature means that you are calm and not agitated, nervous, frantic, or frustrated. To have a peaceful nature means you have a calm emotional climate. If you are calm, patient, and loving, you will bring out the best of this kind of nature in the people around you by being an example of peace. Having a peaceful nature will open the door for other people to become more patient, accepting, and gracious around you. Rather than becoming upset by the ups and downs of your daily life, you will create an environment in which you go with the flow of life. It is easier to make the necessary adjustments to the complications and challenges of life if you have a calm and peaceful nature. By being peaceful, you eliminate many of the mental distractions that interfere with your wisdom and common sense, making it easier for you to see the solutions rather than focusing on the problems.

Develop a Peaceful Nature

The first step in developing a calm and peaceful nature is to acknowledge that this is a priority in your life. Instead of waiting for others to step ahead and blaming them for the chaos in your workplace or home, make the decision to have a peaceful nature as your top priority. Decide that this is the goal worth driving towards, to develop a peaceful, calm nature. Practise the strategies that will bring out a peaceful and calm nature in your heart. You will discover that, when peace is your primary goal, everything else will fall into place. Everything will be much easier to deal with, too. In addition, you will be setting the stage for yourself to live in a peaceful climate and have a peaceful life. This, in turn, further reduces the chaos around your home and workplace. By becoming more peaceful at heart and developing a peaceful nature, you develop a sense of worthiness, and people around you will appreciate you more and see you as a kind-hearted, peaceful person. Becoming more peaceful will not happen overnight, but it is certainly something worth striving for. Beginning now, you can make the choice that you will go towards the direction of calming yourself down and striving towards a calm life.

We should also have gratitude for having a peaceful home. It is remarkable to reflect on how fortunate we are to have a home—a place to rest that has a haven of potential peace in it. We should express our gratitude for having a lovely home despite its imperfections. We still have a home that protects us from the elements of heat and cold. Our home helps to keep us comfortable; yet, for the most part, its value is taken for granted. I have seen the world, from the very poor countries to the very rich. I have seen the grass roots of poverty. I have seen people with no homes, living on the streets in India where I grew up. So, when I see that my family and I have a home, a shelter, I am very thankful, and I feel grateful that I have a peaceful home, one that I should not take for granted. We should be very thankful and have great gratitude for our homes. We should develop peaceful homes and peaceful natures to live in our homes. We should take part in the expression of gratitude for having peaceful homes and developing peaceful natures. Gratitude is a very powerful emotion. It brings out the best in us and helps us maintain our emotional well-being. It also helps us to be happy.

[1.] Ella Wheeler Wilcox, "Solitude," in *Great Short Poems*, edited by Paul Negri (Mineola, NY: Dover Publications, Inc., 2000), 34–35.

CHAPTER 22

Stop Complaining and Start Living

I hold it true, whate'er befall;
I feel it, when I sorrow most;
'T is better to have loved and lost
Than never to have loved at all.
Alfred Lord Tennyson[1]

Alfred Lord Tennyson (1809–1892) was an English Victorian poet. In this poem, he sends us a message that we often ignore: if we live in fear of failing, we do not really live. He is telling us to go on with life as if our potential failure is of no consideration. We should ignore the fears of failure and proceed in life without fear. If we choose the safety of non-commitment rather than risk ourselves in partnerships like marriage, we suffer a great loss. Tennyson's poem expresses this view very well, especially in the last four lines, which I have quoted above. I do not think there is any such thing as failure. We cannot fail, but only produce results of our actions. In any relationship that has "failed" or perhaps resulted in a breakup, the partners have not failed. This is not failure. It is just that they have produced this result from that marriage. We should not jump to the conclusion that we have failed in life if our marriage ends but think just that a particular relationship has produced its result. It is far better to have acted on the results rather than to have lived a life in fear. The word, "fear," means to be apprehensive about a possible situation or event; if we fear failure, we are afraid that our faults or circumstances will limit us, and we feel this fear without evidence, without fear appearing to be based in the real world. In other words, we look at what we imagine to be a strong reason for inaction and then we allow it to become a reality even before we attempt to correct ourselves.

Fear is supported by the illusion that any action is going to fail. That fear means that we think ourselves to be worthless and have the tendency to flee and not fight. But I think it is better to have a supple mind that allows you to accept and adapt. Then, and only then, can you conquer fear. Alfred Lord Tennyson's poem sends a message that you should be willing to make mistakes, even knowing that losing is a possibility. Artificial judgments of failure only keep us from making mistakes, and those mistakes are the very things that encourage inner personal growth. The only real failure is in allowing fear to keep us from acting.

What I have learned from this classic poem is to refuse to entertain the term "fear" or "failure"—about myself or anyone else close to me. I tell them and remind them that, if things do not go as planned, you did not fail. You just must produce the results of your actions and then ask a very powerful question: "What am I going to do with the results that I have produced?" After asking this question, act not in resentment but to improve yourself, so you can produce better results in your next attempt. When others feel that you are a failure, you gently remind them that you have not failed today; rather, you have produced the results of your actions. Every failure is a step forward in your life towards success.

The way out of failure is to face the problem and laugh at the results rather than get embarrassed or intimidated by its outcome. That is the only way to work towards your dreams. We should stop complaining about failures and start living our lives with enthusiasm.

"Stop complaining. Nobody listens to you." You have heard this often. It is quite true that if we complain too much, people will not have to listen to us. In my profession as a doctor, I listen to the complaints of a patient. It is important to listen to their complaints and make a proper diagnosis to give the proper treatment. I have patients in my practice who complain too much, even when they truly do not have a real illness. These patients lose the trust of the doctor. When they get into real trouble, then it is not uncommon for us to think that this particular complaint also may not be a true one. Sometimes, we do not pay, enough attention to them. I have seen some patients who complain of chest pain. They present themselves to emergency departments quite frequently. They may have underlying coronary artery disease, but sometimes, when they have this underlying problem, with every little chest pain that may or may not be angina, they go to emergency. The emergency physician sees these patients, does routine tests, such as an electrocardiogram and cardiac enzymes, and if they are normal, the patient is discharged home. If there is an abnormality, the patient will get a further assessment by a cardiologist. The point I am trying to make here is that, if the complainer complains too many times, he will lose the trust of the doctors. When he or she truly has a problem, the individual may not get the necessary attention, as in the case of patients with coronary artery disease (CAD). I train my patients to use their medications regularly and go to the ER if their nitroglycerine taken sublingually does not work within a reasonable amount of time. Most of my patients with coronary artery disease get coronary angiograms and do know the extent of their disease. Many of these patients with coronary artery disease who get chest pains know it may not be truly angina; their symptoms may be related to chest-wall pains. They assume that it is an angina-like pain, but, due to underlying anxiety, they present to the emergency department too many times and lose the trust of the emergency physicians. It is very important in my profession to explain to patients with coronary artery disease about the importance of their medication and when to go to the emergency department. If the patient truly is having a myocardial infarction, she or he should not ignore it and should get medical attention in the proper amount of time to get the appropriate treatment with thrombolytic therapy (clot busters).

I have observed two persistent dynamics about complainers that I will share with you. First, listening to people complain feels stressful and encourages us to complain ourselves. The other observation is that the complaining never stops. In fact, it seems that it becomes worse if you stop the complainer from complaining. It gives the complainer energy and feeds the cycle that already exists, and therefore the complaining becomes worse. Rather than complaining about complaining, I have decided to make peace with the fact that listening to complaining is a fact of life, and, to be completely honest with you, I have discovered something truly remarkable about this. The complaining has lessened substantially when I listen to the complainer. It is not getting to me nearly as much as it used to. There seems to be far less of it to contend with or to fight with. The fact that I have become less emotionally invested in the complaining has made complaining less appealing to me but more easily tolerated by me if I have to listen to it.

My advice is simple. As difficult as it sounds, and as justified or irrational as your complainer may be, try to stop your part in the process: do not get annoyed by listening to the complaints. My guess is that, if you stop complaining, those complaints that you are forced to listen to will gradually disappear. It is difficult to accept, but complaining is a part of life. Listening to complaints is also a part of life. We have to have open ears to listen to people who complain and take it in stride. You will find very quickly that the complainer will realize how patient you are and will stop complaining because it is not going to take the complainer anywhere by constantly complaining.

The point I am trying to make here is that we have to make ourselves strong enough for the complainer, and stop complaining that we have to listen to the complainer. You will have to learn to harden your emotions somewhat in your system so that you will listen but not react in a forceful way back, or the result will produce more bad feelings with the person who is complaining. With this kind of an attitude—having a cool mind and listening to the complainer with your full attention and then giving your piece of advice with wisdom and thought—you will bring about a change in the complainer, who will eventually stop complaining.

We should start living and embrace the changes in our lives as they come. The fact is, everything is in a constant state of change. Our bodies are changing. Our physical structure, our homes, and environment are changing. Our children are changing and growing up and going through the ongoing state of change—physically and emotionally.

We can provoke and intensify the change, or we can surrender and embrace it and start living rather than resisting the changes. Many people resist change with all their might, and they fight against it. Evolving traditions, the changing attitudes of our children, aging, and virtually all major changes in our lives are never ending. The problem with resisting change is you will lose the battle in time. Change is one of the only certainties in life, one of the few things we can count on. We cannot resist its inevitability. When we try, there is pain and sorrow, and we can miss out on potential joy and happiness. Many people spend so much time and energy fearing age when they reach their later years. It is almost as if they somehow missed the years that preceded because their attention was somewhere else. Some people are so unhappy that their children are growing up and leaving home that they fail to appreciate the year or two during which their son or daughter is home. Still, others get depressed over slight shifts in family traditions.

What I am suggesting here is that you start living and go with the flow of life and become less upset and frustrated over changes over which you have no control. Go ahead and enjoy your life, and don't bother or worry about the next phase. I am not suggesting that you blindly go into the aging process without making the effort to take care of yourself. All I am suggesting is that you go with the flow of life and start living each day, and stop complaining about the things you cannot change. Enjoy the next phase as much as the last one, and open your heart to what is in front of you rather than what has passed by. You will find that adjustment becomes easier if you start living today and accepting the changes that come.

When you embrace change, you open the door of your heart to a more peaceful existence. Rather than insisting that your life be a certain way and that it stays the same way, you will begin a journey that includes acceptance and appreciation in every phase of your life, and you will go with the flow of life. Then, life becomes more of an adventure. Each step you take will seem important and special.

Go with the flow of life.

Start living.

Embrace change as it comes.

This will lead to a happier life.

---

1. Alfred Lord Tennyson, "In Memoriam A. H. H." in *Tennyson: Poems and Plays*, Edited by T. Herbert Warren (London: Oxford University Press. 1971), 237.

CHAPTER 23

Nothing Lasts Forever

> I saw grief drinking a cup of sorrow, and called out, "Tastes sweet, does it not?" "You have got me," grief answered. "And you have ruined my business. How can I sell sorrow when you know it is a blessing?"
> *Jalaluddin Rumi*[1]

Jalaluddin Rumi (1207–1273) was a Persian Sufi saint, poet, and mystic who wrote about pure love beyond ego. This love will lead, he said, to a union with the divine. Rumi was a 13th century poet who lived in the area known as the Sultanate of Rum (today in Turkey), and he sends this message from 800 years ago. It suggests that grief is a blessing rather than something that is bad or evil. It is necessary to understand that grief has a sweet nectar that is available to us in our dark moments in life.

Grieving is important. We all react to tragic news or events, and grieving seems to be a natural way to react to the experiences of pain and suffering in our lives. But, if we take the wisdom of Rumi, whose words tell us that the grief is sweet, grief actually becomes a blessing in disguise that will propel us towards a higher level of consciousness. The dark moments of our lives provide us with this kind of energy that will propel us to a higher level of consciousness. Therefore, we should take grief not as painful but as something to incorporate with wisdom; this will generate the necessary energy to move us to a higher consciousness instead of having grief sink us into despair. We are then able to move to a higher level of consciousness with a higher level of energy.

For example, if we are in pain or are suffering most of us sink with sorrow and feel the need to tell everyone about our misfortunes. (The pain might be caused by any number of things: some kind of accident or illness in the family, a financial disaster, a marriage break up or even the break up of friends, a fire, a flood, a loss of property, or a death that leads to the stages of anger, denial, and finally grief.) Later, we slowly begin to rise and reach a level of acceptance.

Now, if we take Rumi's words of wisdom and place them in our life, word telling us that "grief is a blessing," instead of grieving with sorrow, we will function at a higher level of awareness and feel wise and blessed. Whenever we fall to the lowest, we will find the inner strength if we take this wisdom to heart and work with it. There is an intelligent system that we are all an inseparable part of. We have to learn, right now, in the middle of sorrow, to take this lesson to heart and say that sorrow or grief "is sweet" because it has put us on a higher level of consciousness. The grief actually tastes sweet rather than bitter.

There is something to learn right here—sorrow is sweet and we are going to drink it and ruin the day of those who believe that grief is forever. We have societies living even today who believe that grief and mourning do not question the divine timing of a person's arrival on this earth or the divine timing of a person's departure from this world. We all know that everything is in order, and, if we take this wisdom that gives comfort and see the perfection of our universe, we will experience the divine spirit flowing through every part of this creation; it is even in many of the painful experiences you have had over time. Take comfort and strength from this intelligent system working through this world and celebrate this functioning of a perfect system.

When we know that grief and sorrow are blessings and all losses are a part of the divine order, then we gradually sweeten the sorrow, and we will gain the energy to go to a higher level in all areas of our lives, with acceptance.

Nothing lasts forever. Everything comes to an end. For instance, you anticipate something and the next thing you know, it is over, and then you look forward to another event. There is an enormous freedom in remembering the spirit of this wisdom. The fact is that the foundation of this wisdom is a very peaceful life. It serves as a reminder that everything has its time. There are seasons, which come and go. There is a time and place for everything. Understanding this wisdom gives us perspective during hard times: nothing lasts forever. This wisdom also gives us hope and confidence that we will get through the event, that it will pass as it always does. We look forward to the next event. For example, when we have young children, we think they may never grow up, but the fact is, the children do grow up and get on with their lives. We grow old, and, ultimately, we all are very mortal and pass on. Therefore, we should take this wisdom to heart and understand that nothing is forever.

Everything passes on.

If we are going through a crisis, we feel we will never get through it. But somehow we find a way. If you have a big fight with your spouse, you may swear that you will never forgive or forget, but eventually you will find that your heart loves again, and you forget, and things move on. In the midst of a particular day you may feel as if you are overwhelmed and everything seems to take much longer. But eventually the schedule gets back to normal. Time and again we struggle, but we do move on.

Everything passes on.

As we look back on our lives, we see that all things come and go like the seasons—winter, spring, summer, and fall. In the same way, we have joy, sorrow, praise, and blame; hardship, ease, rest, and exhaustion; accomplishments and mishaps. All things happen. They come and go. Genuine freedom and happiness come when we see this dynamic in our lives. We may go through something difficult, but it will pass on. Therefore, this wisdom—that nothing lasts forever—is very important, and we can learn a lot from this wisdom. In this way, we can keep our perspective in the midst of chaos, knowing that nothing lasts forever, everything passes on, it comes and goes and allows us to keep our perspective and an open heart, and even a sense of humour during chaotic phases of our lives.

Whenever we feel stressed or bothered, whenever we are going through a critical or difficult time, we should always keep this wisdom in mind: that life is short, and the difficult phases of life pass on. Nothing stays the same forever. The most effective way to maintain a grateful spirit and keep us from being overwhelmed is to remember that all things are in a phase of change. Even the hard times are never present forever, and they do pass as part of the phases of life.

> Every time a value is born, existence takes on a new meaning; every time one dies, some part of that meaning passes away.
> *Joseph Wood Krutch*[2]

When you develop this wisdom that everything is mortal, that nothing stays the same forever, then you change yourself, and you also don't take any person for granted. It is commonly seen that it is the people you see the most that you take for granted, for example, your spouse and children. It is so easy to get lost in your own world that you begin to believe that your spouse has a much easier life than you do.

You forget how hard your spouse works for you. There is a tendency to think our jobs are more important than our spouses' work. We take our partners in marriage for granted. This tendency can create a great deal of dissent, and this tendency is, to a large degree, preventable. The key to prevention is to put yourself in your spouse's shoes and see how you feel. If we have the wisdom to say that everything changes and passes on and nothing stays forever, we can also develop the wisdom to not take our partners for granted.

If we try as a mental exercise to change our roles and put ourselves in our spouses' shoes, then we will recognize how important it is to not take our loved ones for granted, regardless of our personal situations. Even if you and your partner both work and both help out at home, it can be enormously helpful to experiment with the strategy of changing roles as a mental exercise. Through this experience, you will develop an appreciation for each other and all that both of you do. We should always keep in mind the wisdom of the changing patterns and phases of life and the simple fact that, as humans, we are very mortal. Everything changes. Nothing lasts forever. With this simple philosophy, we can appreciate each other and develop more love and affection at home.

Last, I would like to discuss very briefly that there is always something you can do to improve yourself, no matter whether you are rich or poor, where you live, what you do, or how much money you have. No amount of complaining, simply wishing for things to happen, or clever planning will ever change this simple fact of life.

> If we all did the things we are capable of doing, we would literally astound ourselves.
> *Thomas A. Edison*[3]

Step back and realize how easy it is to let things get out of hand if you always have something else on your mind or if you always have something to do. If you decide you won't rest until everything is done, you will probably spend your whole life tired and frustrated. If you have the philosophy and wisdom to understand that life is an ongoing adventure with phases and to know that nothing stays the same forever, then you can see and understand that the best thing you can hope to do is to stay on top of things. Decide what is truly important to you and maintain a sense of goodwill and humour. In short, you can only do what you can do in the amount of time you have.

After coming to the realization that what is pervasive in our lives is the fact that we will never be able to get everything done, we can be happy. Otherwise we will always feel defeated. We need only acknowledge that, if we are doing one thing, then we aren't doing something else. Therefore, we can start today by giving ourselves a break and understanding that we can only do so much. We need to learn to prioritise, to figure out what is more important to do during a particular phase of life and do that particular thing and enjoy it. Always keep in mind that life has phases and everything passes on. Nothing lasts forever. This simple strategy and wisdom will make you more humble and a happier person.

---

1. Jalaluddin Rumi, quoted in Wayne Dyer, *Wisdom of the Ages: 60 Days to Enlightenment* (New York: Harper Collins Publishers, Inc., 1998), 24.
2. Joseph Wood Krutch, *The Modern Temper* (New York, 1929), 94.
3. Thomas A. Edison, quoted in Anthony Robbins, *Awaken the Giant Within* (New York: Simon & Schuster, 1992), 431.

CHAPTER 24

Meditation

This book would not be complete without a chapter on meditation.

> Meditation means creating a continual familiarity with a virtuous object in order to transform your mind. Merely understanding some point does not transform your mind. You may intellectually see the advantages of an altruistic awakening mind, but that does not actually affect your self-centered attitude. Your self-centeredness will be dispelled only through constantly familiarizing yourself with that understanding. This is what is meant by meditation.
>
> Meditation can be of two types: *Analytical meditation* uses analysis and reflection, whereas in *single-pointed meditation*, the mind dwells on whatever has been understood. When you meditate on love and compassion, you try to cultivate such an attitude in your mind, thinking, *May all sentient beings be free from suffering*. On the other hand, when you meditate on emptiness or impermanence, you take impermanence or emptiness as the object of your meditation.
> *Dalai Lama*[1]

The current interest in meditation is no longer just a cultural curiosity. Physicians are now prescribing meditation as we are becoming more and more aware of its benefits. Meditation has been shown to slow down the process of chronic diseases, such as heart conditions, AIDS, cancer, and infertility. It also has been used to restore balance in the face of such psychiatric disturbances as depression, hyperactivity, and ADD (attention deficit disorder).

In Eastern mysticism and Western science, doctors are embracing meditation, not because they think it is cool but rather because scientific studies are beginning to show that it works particularly well for stress-related conditions. More than 30 years of meditation research has told us that meditation works beautifully as an antidote to stress.

Wisdom comes in silence.
Buddha[2]

The Buddhist philosophy believes that sitting in silence for 10 to 40 minutes a day, while actively concentrating on a breath or a word or an image, can train your mind to focus on the present over the past and future, allowing you to transcend reality by fully accepting it. In most modern forms, meditation has dropped all of the old ways of mantras and now simply involves just sitting quietly and focusing on something and saying a phrase or syllable, fully focusing on a sound or on your breathing itself. It is a practice of repeating the same sound, such as "oomm," which can produce a soothing effect.

Meditation is an ancient discipline, but scientists have only recently developed tools that are sensitive enough to see what goes on in our brain when we do meditation.

Even when people are meditating for the first time, the act of meditation will create a reduction in the beta wave, a sign that the cortex is not processing information as actively as usual. After the first 20-minute session, patients show a marked decrease in the beta wave activity, shown in the frontal lobe of the brain. The frontal lobe is the most highly evolved part of the brain responsible for reasoning, planning, emotions, and self-conscious awareness. During meditation, the frontal cortex tends to go off-line.

The parietal lobe of the brain is that part of the brain which processes sensory information about the surrounding world, orienting you in time and space. During meditation, activity in the parietal lobe also slows down. The thalamus of the brain is the gatekeeper for the senses. This organ focuses your attention by funnelling some sensory data deeper into the brain, and it stops other signals in their tracks. Meditation reduces the flow of incoming information to a very slow trickle.

Reticular formation acts the part of the brain's sentry. This structure receives incoming stimuli and puts the brain on alert to respond. Meditation sends back the arousal signal. It has been scientifically proven that meditation does work.

How To Meditate

First, find a quiet place and turn out all bright lights. The fewer distractions you have, the easier it is to concentrate. Close your eyes. The idea is to shut out the outside world so your brain can stop actively processing information coming from all the senses. Pick a word—any word: find a word or phrase that means something to you whose sound or rhyme is soothing when repeated. Say it again and again, the same word or phrase. Try to say your word or phrase to yourself with every out-breath. The monotony will help you focus.

After training in meditation for 8 weeks, subjects show a pronounced change in brain wave patterns, shifting from an alpha wave pattern of aroused conscious thought, to the theta wave pattern; the theta wave dominates the brain during periods of deep relaxation.

Meditation has become a field of great interest in modern times. In March 2004, the Dalai Lama met with Western-trained psychologists and neuroscientists in India to attend the Mind and Life Institute, which organized studies of highly accomplished meditation masters using the most advanced imaging technology. The results were discussed at various Mind and Life conferences, especially the one co-sponsored by Johns Hopkins and the Georgetown University Medical Center. This 2005 conference, "Mind and Life XIII," was entitled "The Science and Clinical Applications of Meditation." Not only did these studies and conferences allow for a more detailed understanding of how the brain works during meditation, but they also provide a lot of insight into the research on meditation.

What scientists are discovering through these studies is that, with enough practice, the neurons of the brain will adapt themselves to direct activity in that frontal concentration-oriented area of the brain.

> All man's misery is derived from not being able to sit quietly in a room alone.
> *Blaise Pascal*[3]

It is important to have contentment and inner peace. Think how many people would start meditating if you could convince them that they would live longer without having to go jogging or eat vegetables all of their lives. More than a decade ago, Dr. Dean Ornish showed that meditation, along with yoga and dieting, reversed the build up of plaque in the coronary arteries. In April 2003, at the meeting of the American College of the Urological Association, he announced his most recent findings—

meditation may slow prostate cancer. While his results were interesting, it is important to note that those patients were also dieting and doing yoga.

John Kabat-Zinn, who studied Buddhism in the 1960's and founded the Stress Reduction Clinic at University of Massachusetts Medical Center in 1979, has been trying to find a more scientific demonstration of the healing power of meditation. Over the years, he has helped more than 14,000 people manage their pain without medication. He teaches them to focus on what their pain feels like and accept it rather than fight it. These people have AIDS, cancer, and chronic pain from different diseases.

There is growing evidence from research demonstrating the health benefits of meditation. One study shows that women who meditate and use guided imagery have higher levels of immune cells known to combat tumours in the breast. In addition, many studies, have established that meditation can significantly reduce blood pressure. Given that 60 per cent of doctor visits are the result of stress-related conditions, this evidence may provide some further potential use for meditation. It is not surprising that meditation can sometimes be used to replace Viagra. I hope this does not put Pfizer Pharmaceutical Company out of business, but I believe meditation does work in erectile dysfunction.

Meditation does more than reduce stress. It brings harmony and improves our focus. Although I do not meditate as religiously as I should, whenever I do take time out to do meditation for even 5 to 10 minutes, I feel a great difference in myself. I feel refreshed after meditation.

I highly recommend meditation to my patients, especially those with chronic illnesses, chronic pain, and cancer and also to those with underlying psychological disorders like anxiety and depression.

> Learn to be silent. Let your quiet mind listen and absorb.
> *Pythagoras*[4]

Pythagoras's recommendation from 2,500 years ago specifies the value of silence and meditation. His message points out that, in order to shed our miseries, we must learn to sit silently in a room, alone, and meditate. It is estimated by a renowned psychologist that an average person has about 60,000 separate thoughts each and every day. The problem is that when we have the same 60,000 thoughts yesterday, today, and tomorrow, our minds are filled with the same chatter of day-to-day living. We should learn to be quiet and meditate, which involves learning how to enter the spaces between those thoughts and find a sense of total peace and calm.

However, if we are bombarded by negative thoughts and emotions, which are more common than positive thoughts and emotions, then there is extreme chatter. There is no space between the thoughts; and because there is no space between those thoughts, then there is no peace. This problem of being bombarded with thoughts and emotions leads to suffering and unhappiness. Most of us have minds that race at full speed. We usually have negative thoughts or dialogues in our minds, about money matters, sexual fantasies, our schedules, our children's problems, vacation plans, aging parents, or even the smaller things such as errands to run, weeding the garden, and so on. These perpetual thoughts drain us completely and take the beauty out of ordinary lives.

Therefore, it is very important that the mental pattern should be calm. There should be spaces in between those thoughts—spaces of peace and love. These spaces can be produced by sitting quietly in a room and meditating.

What makes music? It is actually the silence between the notes that makes the music. If there is no silence, no gaps between the notes, then there is only noise. This is well known to many musicians. The same applies to us: when we have no gaps or silences between our thoughts, there will be only noise and confusion.

Pythagoras was an ancient teacher and philosopher who recommended that we should practise quieting our minds and learn to "absorb" so that confusion will disappear and enlightenment or spirituality will come to us. Meditation also affects the quality of our life. It increases our sense of well-being, and it causes an increase in our energy levels, which, in turn, leads to higher productivity at a more conscious level.

Our mind is like a pond. On the surface, there is some disturbance, but deep below the surface, there is stillness or calm. By going below the surface, we come to the spaces between our thoughts, and we are able to enter these gaps. The gap is total emptiness or silence, and it is invisible. No matter how many times we cut through the silence, we still get silence. This can be achieved by meditation.

Therefore, I believe that, if we practice meditation, we may, perhaps, reach the divine.

1. Dalai Lama, *Core Teachings of Tibetan Buddhism* (San Francisco: Harper Collins Publishers, 1995), 51.
2. Buddha, *Complete Works of Swami Abhedananda* (Calcutta: Ramakrishna Vedanta Math, 1969), 592.
3. Blaise Pascal, quoted in Wayne W. Dyer, *Wisdom of the Ages: 60 Days to Enlightenment* (New York: Harper Collins Publishers, Inc., 1998), 1.
4. Pythagoras, quoted in Wayne W. Dyer, *Wisdom of the Ages: 60 Days to Enlightenment* (New York: Harper Collins Publishers, Inc., 1998), 2.